The Fly
AND
the Fish

*Angling Instructions
and Reminiscences*

John Atherton

New Foreword by Mike Valla

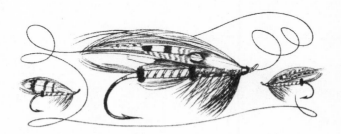

Skyhorse Publishing

Skyhorse Publishing books may be purchased in bulk at special discounts for sales promotion, corporate gifts, fund-raising, or educational purposes. Special editions can also be created to specifications. For details, contact the Special Sales Department, Skyhorse Publishing, 307 West 36th Street, 11th Floor, New York, NY 10018 or info@skyhorsepublishing.com.

Skyhorse® and Skyhorse Publishing® are registered trademarks of Skyhorse Publishing, Inc.®, a Delaware corporation.

Visit our website at www.skyhorsepublishing.com.

10 9 8 7 6 5 4 3 2 1

Library of Congress Cataloging-in-Publication Data is available on file.

Cover design by Brian Peterson

Cover photo credit John Atherton

Print ISBN: 978-1-5107-0753-5

Ebook ISBN: 978-1-5107-0754-2

Printed in the United States of America

TO

MY WIFE

AND BEST

FISHING

COMPANION

Contents

Foreword

Over sixty-five years have passed since John Atherton's now classic *The Fly and the Fish* was first published, yet the amazing intensity and scope of his narrative is still admired. Of all the hundreds of fly-fishing books and articles that fill my bookshelves, and that I've read and enjoyed countless times over the past fifty years, *The Fly and the Fish* still stands as my favorite amongst them. The original 1951 Macmillan edition occupies a special place front and center on my shelf when it's not back on my nightstand.

Contemporary flyfishermen and flyfisherwomen, too, have discovered and rediscovered Atherton's epic work, sending new followers and recruits on searches for the original printing or the later Dover reprint that first appeared in 1971. The recent resurgence of both national and international interest in John Atherton's unique observations and theories surrounding fly pattern design and style alone call for this new Skyhorse printing. But this tome offers so much more than simple theories.

My own appreciation and interest in John Atherton and *The Fly and the Fish* began in the late 1960s and early 1970s. Those were the years when, as a boy, I stayed with Walt and Winnie Dette at their home and fly shop in Roscoe, New York, during the fishing season. The Dettes were part of the so-called Catskill Mountains region school of fly tiers, artisans who practiced their craft near some of the most famous trout streams in America—the Beaverkill, Neversink, Schoharie, and Willowemoc among them. The Dettes, along with other Catskill school fly tiers such as Rube Cross, Harry and Elsie Darbee, Ed Hewitt, and Art Flick are all mentioned in *The Fly and the Fish*. Their favorite rivers within the region are also mentioned in Atherton's pages.

Readers will learn that Atherton dedicated the last chapter of *The Fly and the Fish* to his own favorite river, the Battenkill in Vermont, on whose banks he eventually built his house in the late 1940s. However, he was still very much a part of the Catskill fly-fishing story, and very much admired by the time I first fished the region's rivers.

Atherton's name surfaced from time to time around both the Dettes' fly shop and the Darbees' shop up the road. Somewhere between the ribald jokes, adult humor that my young ears shouldn't have been exposed to, and the more serious fly fishing chatter that filled the fly shops and river banks in those years I first heard Atherton's name. Hanging on the wall at the bottom of the staircase in the old Dette house were the color illustrations painted by Atherton of trout flies that appeared in John McDonald's May 1946 *Fortune*, now classic, magazine piece titled "Trout Fishing and Trout Flies." It was impossible not admire Atherton's art on the way upstairs to my bedroom.

The beautiful paintings that appeared in the *Fortune* article featured all the Catskill classic dry flies—Quill Gordon, Light Cahill, and Hendrickson, among others. The Dettes, the Darbees, and other members of the Catskill school and beyond were named beneath each fly illustration. While John Atherton admired and painted the standard Catskill fly patterns and additional flies mentioned in his book, he had his own ideas concerning fly design. His profound theories found their way into *The Fly and the Fish*.

I can't recall with certainty exactly when I first acquired a copy of his book, but my guess is it would have been in the early 1970s. By the time I read *The Fly and the Fish*, I was already quite aware from my Catskill fly-fishing upbringing, that Atherton was also a famous artist by profession. Aided by the influence of contemporary, neighbor, and friend Norman Rockwell, Atherton's paintings covered magazines such as the *Saturday Evening Post* and *Fortune*. His art hung in the most prestigious museums and galleries in the county, yet his artistic gift was expressed in other ways beyond painting.

What John Atherton did with fly patterns was brave if not ingenious: he linked the principles of the impressionistic school of artists to dry fly, wet fly, and nymph design. His chapter titled "Flies and Impressionism" blew me away the first time I read it, and it still blows me away after many re-readings. Connecting the impressionistic art of Monet and Renoir to trout flies is a powerful, yet enlightening, approach to fly pattern design.

There is no doubt that this timely reprinting of *The Fly and the Fish* will inspire and edify readers after they're exposed to and entertained by John Atherton's unique mix of fascinating concepts, practical instructions, and enjoyable stories that fill the book's pages. Chapters sharing his times fishing for Atlantic salmon on the famous Miramichi in New Brunswick, steelhead on the Klamath in California, and the trout on Ed Hewitt's Neversink in the Catskills will capture the imagination.

I write these final words in my "Atherton Room," a small cabin near the Battenkill, John Atherton's beloved river. My friend Wally Murray owns and lives in Atherton's old house on the banks of the stream, a couple of miles from this place, in a cabin called "Vallahalla." When Wally visits, we chat about the old Battenkill River days and Atherton's work.

The Atherton Room is decorated with everything Atherton—with photos of him on one wall and framed pictures of his original flies that he tied on another. Hackle capes—cree and grizzly and furnace shades—that once belonged to John Atherton sit on a shelf. That famous framed print of a leaping salmon sits over the bed. The old *Fortune* magazine issue with those marvelous fly plates I remembered since boyhood sits on the nightstand along with a second copy of *The Fly and the Fish*. A walnut block letter sign above the room door entry announces to visitors "Atherton."

To say that John Atherton has influenced me would be an understatement. He's been a large part of my own writings, efforts that are undertaken to ensure that he's not forgotten. It is my fervent hope that readers will also appreciate John Atherton and his seminal work—*The Fly and the Fish*.

—Mike Valla, Ballston Spa, New York, 2016

Introduction

IN less than a year after the first publication of *The Fly and The Fish* John Atherton unexpectedly died of a heart attack. I knew him as a fine artist and sportsman, a devoted husband, and an amusing fishing companion with a delightful sense of humor and exclamatory zest for life. His family and friends called him Jack.

Several years before Jack died, a staff member of the Museum of Modern Art in New York City listed his paintings, which were on exhibition there, under the heading of Magic Realism. And I thought it was an exceptionally poignant analogy of not only his abstract compositions of reality on canvas but of his conception of life in general.

Yes, Jack was a romantic realist, and his exuberant outbursts of wonder over any natural phenomenon helped me to see this Earth of ours as the magical place it really is.

But the first chapter of the book reveals his true character better than I can, and it gives the reader some idea of the character of another sensitive man devoted to the art of fly fishing. He is John MacDonald, the author and scholar now well known to anglers everywhere. Further on in the book Jack mentions Harold Gillum, whom we met while living in Ridgefield, Connecticut, and who preferred to be called by his nickname, Pinkie.

He built marvelous flyrods, and refused to produce them in mass production, so there are relatively few in existence. Each rod he made of especially selected bamboo and with a specific angler in mind. I know a man who compares his Gillum trout rod to a Stradivarius violin.

Pinkie and Jack enjoyed many a day fishing together, and I recall Pinkie saying that he would rather sit on the bank and watch

Jack cast a dry fly than fish, himself. Both of them were perfectionists, and they never seemed to tire of discussing the art of building the perfect flyrod.

Much of the text of *The Fly and the Fish* was developed through discussions between Pinkie Gillum, John MacDonald, Edward Hewitt, Alfred Miller ("Sparse Grey Hackle" who edited the book) and Jack. And to prove some of his theories Jack did some experiments with Mr. Hewitt.

I remember one in that fabulous Hewitt house at Grammercy Park in New York City. It was the first time I had been there, so Mr. Hewitt showed us around the house. His workshop was on the fifth floor and the work benches were stacked with hundreds of tools he had accumulated over a period of many years. A trout reel that he had been making was lying on a workbench, and Jack picked it up and admired it. (He later bought it for me and now it is a collector's item.)

Mr. Hewitt next led us down to the fourth floor, to his lab, which was a confusion of chemistry equipment, odd boxes, Bunsen burners, glass jars, test tubes, all sorts of odd things. He explained that he had been doing research on vitamins and trace minerals in natural foods, which he believed would prolong life if they were included in our diets.

It was just another one of his hobbies, and at the time I didn't appreciate how important it was, or how far ahead of the times he was. I suppose his interest in nutrition and vitamins stemmed from the research he did for the fish in his hatchery at the Neversink. Perhaps I've dwelled too long on Mr. Hewitt's hobbies, but Jack's admiration for him was endless, and I am using him as an illustration of how fascinating life can become for an angler after the age of retirement.

Finally Mr. Hewitt led us down to his personal apartment on the third floor, and the two rooms there were more astonishing than the lab. I vaguely recall a pulley on the ceiling over his bed, and various contraptions attached to it. One was a large piece of plywood, to keep out drafts, he said, when the windows were open, and he could lower it to the floor while lying in bed. Indeed, the interior of that entire old Victorian house would have afforded Rube Goldberg a wealth of material for his cartoons.

Introduction

Mr. Hewitt's sitting room was crowded with an aquarium of small fish, a glass tank of water, furniture, and piles of books. He and Jack stopped in front of the glass tank and began discussing what a trout saw when looking up at a Mayfly on the surface.

Their theories were too technical for me, so I browsed through the books, books about fishing, fish hatcheries, protein hay, vitamins, lecithin, all sorts of odd subjects relating in one way or another to the inventions and writings of that versatile old gentleman.

Then, at the sound of Jack's convulsed laughter, I joined them again. Over by the glass tank those two characters were down on their knees, upside-down on the floor, peering up through the water in the tank, looking at a couple of dry flies, which were floating on surface film. The gymnastics were being performed, I learned, to get a fish-eye view of the flies, and to check Jack's theories about the "light pattern" artificials make on and under the water. What fun! But that was a long time ago.

Now, I treasure my Atherton flies, Hewitt reels and Gillum rods. Jack's impressionistic fly patterns have worked wonders for me, have fooled trout in rivers around the United States, Europe, Canada, even in Labrador where I least expected to find May flies—and did.

I still have a few of his Spiders (described in Chapter VIII), and these flies can never be replaced. He tied them of very stiff hackles, which stand up on surface film and when twitched skate the Spider over the water in a manner that seems to infuriate trout. Especially large trout, and even salmon sometimes, are inclined to strike furiously at Spiders.

The hackles are exceptionally tough because they came from a chicken that had been raised by another dedicated fly fisherman who ties his own flies. Willis Stauffer, whom we called Chip, kept his chickens outdoors in all kinds of weather and in a vast enclosure of wire mesh, where they, like wild birds, flew around the yard and roosted in trees. Rather an expensive hobby, I thought, but for the chicken neck from which Jack got the hackles for his Spiders he exchanged an original Atherton painting! Of course to appreciate such an exchange one must be an angler and just as delightfully crazy as those two were.

Jack not only supplied me with flies, he balanced my rods with fishing lines and leaders, so after his death, and after the lines he had made wore out, I had trouble finding lines I could cast as well. But now that nylon lines have taken the place of silk, and weight-forward lines are on the market, I have less trouble. And it wouldn't surprise me to learn that the designers had read Chapter XIII of *The Fly and the Fish* before developing the tapers for the new WF lines.

Unless it has a weighted core, an aircel line weighs less than a silk one of the same size and taper so to get the same weight forward the designers had to have a larger diameter toward the end. I can't cast my weight forward lines as far out as the silk ones Jack spliced together for me, but if I cut approximately three feet from the taper, or almost down to the largest diameter at the fly end, I have less trouble.

The large diameter at the end doesn't necessarily result in a clumsy presentation of a fly to a fish; expert casters use a technique that shoots out the line so the fly alights, and then the leader, on to the water well ahead of the line. There has been tremendous improvements in the tapers of lines the past few years. Perhaps by next year the designers will have improved them even more.

Fiberglass rods have become very popular since Jack wrote *The Fly and the Fish*. Even I have succumbed. Mine are hollow, have no metal ferrules, are nine feet long, and weigh quite a bit less than my Gillum salmon rods the same length. Surely Jack would approve if he were alive; my arm isn't as strong as it was when I was young.

My nine-foot Gillum rods shoot a fly further out, but not for long, because I get too tired to cast properly. And certainly bamboo holds its power longer than fiberglass.

Lee Cuddy, the noted salt-water flyfisher in Florida, balanced two of my glass rods with WF aircel lines, and he cut off almost all of the fine taper from the end of each, and although the rods are the same length, one has faster action than the other, so he chose a different size line for each. Thus proving to me that I should never again buy a line until I had tried it, or one like it, on my rod. One is a floating line, for bonefish, and one has a sinking tip, for tarpon. I use the floating line when fishing for salmon with a dry fly, and the one with a sinking tip when fishing for salmon with a wet fly in fairly deep water.

Also, since Jack wrote the book nylon leader material has taken the place of gut. And while tying a leader of nylon I follow Jack's specifications, as given in Chapter XIII, and to get a more gradual taper from the large diameter at the end of a line to the leader, I tie—with a nail knot—a piece of forty-pound test monofilament, as instructed by Joe Brooks, on to the end of the line.

Of course there have been changes in fishing equipment the past nineteen years, and I believe if Jack were alive he would be one of the first to keep his tackle up to date. And so would Edward Hewitt. He loved to experiment with new materials.

I miss him too. He was in his early nineties when he died, after a major operation. The last time I talked to him was in the hospital, the night before the operation, and he seemed full of life. We talked about Jack, and then about the Eskimos in Labrador, with whom I'd lived and fished the past summer. Having adopted the white man's diet, which consisted mostly of hardtack, white bread, tea and sugar, almost every one of them was suffering from malnutrition.

Mr. Hewitt said that when he got out of the hospital he would send to me the names of vitamins and minerals to replace the deficiencies in their diet.

Recalling that often during his later years Mr. Hewitt had said he had so much to do he didn't have time to die, I believed he would get out of that hospital alive.

And his parting remark was: "I'm very anxious for them to get it over with," and then, his eyes twinkling merrily, he added, "so I can get back on my feet and take you fishing at the Neversink next summer."

But he didn't make it. And the ashes of my old friend, who had been known as the Dean of Fishermen, were sprinkled into the Neversink, as he had requested.

Several years later Pinkie Gillum died of a heart attack at his home in Connecticut. Now, collectors are offering large sums for his rods.

And Jack, who was too young to die, had frequently said that when his time came he hoped it would be when he was in fishing waders. That is how it was, on the shore of his beloved Miramichi River in Canada.

Then, at home in Vermont two of his fishing companions, Lee Wulff and Walter Squires, helped me bury his ashes under the root of a young maple on the bank of the Battenkill. Today Jack's ashes rest beside a pool from which he had caught and released a large brownie each fishing season we lived there.

And I can only be thankful he has been spared the knowledge that pollution has ruined almost every trout stream in Vermont, that his "favorite trout stream" is now stocked with pale limp hatchery fish each year, that pollution in the Miramichi is driving Atlantic salmon away from that whole great system of rivers, that another wonderful species of wildlife, Atlantic salmon, is facing world-wide extinction, and that our daughter and the majority of young people around the world are rightly irate and concerned about the pollution of air and water, which just might exterminate mankind during their lifetime.

I am sorry to end on such a gloomy note. But that is how it is today. A tragic reality. And instead of lighting an eternal flame on Jack's grave I have been supporting in every way possible any movement that strives to conserve—or to bring back to this Earth all which ruthless pillage destroyed—the magic Jack extolled.

MAXINE ATHERTON

Preface

OVER a historic tavern in downtown New York are snug, comfortable quarters where fishermen gather. For many years the Anglers' Club of New York has offered food and conversation to those who, ensconced at the Long Table, prefer the discussion of angling to the reports of the market.

There I have enjoyed a unique companionship. The propounding of new ideas, the recounting of old exploits make happy the hours out of season; and when the May fly is on, late reports, even though touched occasionally with the exaggeration of enthusiasm, provide contact with the march of events at the streamside. It would be an unusual angler indeed who could fail to profit by such an association. I am no exception. When this book was suggested and its theories offered for discussion, I found helpful criticism and encouragement without flattery.

And I found there the patient assistance, tempered with challenging and occasionally vitriolic comment, of Alfred W. Miller—"Sparse Grey Hackle"—in editing and preparing the copy for publication. Without his unflagging efforts this book would have been impossible.

I also wish to acknowledge the generous help of John MacDonald, author of "The Complete Fly Fisherman: The Letters of Theodore Gordon," who gave freely of his time and intellectual equipment to help me with a perplexing writing problem when he had more profitable things to do.

It is with trepidation that I cast this, my first literary fly, into the stream of angling. But knowing anglers as I do, it is my hope that I shall find more consideration among them than I would among ordinary mortals. After all, I am a fisherman too!

CHAPTER I *"Birth of an Idea"*

THE RIVER flowed smooth and dark beneath the fringing alders. Here and there on the surface little rings broke the reflections and occasionally a splash showed white against the bank. A boy was lying prone, peering over the grass into the clear water. His breath came quickly as he saw a big tail appear in the center of a ring, waving slowly from side to side before it quietly sank again.

There was life in the air as well; tiny gauze-winged forms were rising and dipping over the water, sometimes lightly touching its smooth surface. The boy looked upward to watch them. He raised himself and grasped an alder branch for support. He felt a delicate touch on his hand and, turning, saw the insect resting there, its wings slowly opening and closing.

It was an exquisite creature. The wings were nearly transparent, of iridescent pearly color. The up-curved body was shaded darker on the back, tapering to the slender whisks of a tail long and curved. The eyes protruded prominently and were colored a wonderful violet. It held out its long front legs in an almost supplicating attitude, and all its legs were marked with color, speckled and delicately shaded.

What an incredibly beautiful thing, he thought. No wonder trout rose to it so avidly. He looked up at the branch again. There were several of those lovely flies resting there, and one seemed different from the others.

The boy stood up and looked more closely. He saw an insect, darker and duller in color, its back split down the middle, and from its body was emerging another, the delicate, bright one he had already seen. With a sudden movement, it pulled itself clear. The wings were not erect but

1

seemed to be folded close to the back. As he watched, he saw them begin to open. The metamorphosis took place quickly before his eyes, and in a few moments there was another fly, complete, shining, drying itself in the sun. He looked away and when his eyes returned again it was gone. The splashes in the stream continued.

It is no wonder that, with the impact of that introduction, I became a fly fisherman. Surely, I thought, an art based on imitations of such lovely, fragile creatures must offer a great deal, especially if the angler could create them after his own fashion.

When I first studied with my glass the May flies I found, the impression was one of wonder at their beautiful colors. This was followed by a question: "Why, then, were not artificial flies just as beautiful?" Since that memorable occasion, the fascination of attempting to answer the question has never left me, although experience has proved that the answer is not simple.

The category of anglers includes a wide variety of individuals. Angling is an art that appeals to many types, whether young or old, fat or lean, the artisan or the politician, the philosopher or the artist. So it is not unusual to find one like myself, a painter, among their ranks. The study of art brings with it a new regard for visual things, a sharpened observation. This goes well in angling. The angler is necessarily observant and, if successful, has usually succeeded in putting his findings to practical use. As artist and angler, since that early day when I first looked closely at a May fly, I have been acutely aware of the color and texture of trout flies. The art of tying flies is closely related to painting. For me, the change of pace from the picture, which is two-dimensional, to the fly of three dimensions offers the variety of a good hobby. Tying flies, like painting, is a constant series of experiments. It has been fascinating, over the years, to apply the creative urge to an object which may catch a trout as well as afford the satisfaction of invention.

What is it that trout flies attempt to do? When the angler uses flies to catch trout he is offering them a lure that the trout must mistake for some form of food. The fly is based primarily on the imitation, approximation or simulation of an insect or some other small underwater form. Fly tiers have found certain things in their flies to be effective. Some forms are better than others, some colors more deadly. Tiers have produced flies by the millions—and anglers have caught trout on them. But they seldom have asked themselves why some flies are better than others.

The school of art known as "Impressionism" was the result of an inquiry by a group of painters into the reasons for certain effects in nature and how to achieve those effects with paint. They found that an object or form could be more suggestive of life and movement containing the reflections and influences of its surroundings when painted with broken color made up of the pure tones of the spectrum. These artists taught us to see how light affects the forms in nature, building their pictures with small spots of bright color which together gave the effect of light playing upon the form. We then became aware that to copy the exact color of an object gives the effect of a dead thing, and that color must be alive and breathing, like the form itself, or the picture will lack the fundamental qualities inherent in nature. There is no reason why anglers should not profit by such reasoning, and I feel that they have neglected an important field of experimentation in their imitations of natural insects. Later in this book, I shall present the results of my observations and experiments in developing the impressionistic theory for trout flies, using the broken color principle of the impressionist painters.

While the magnifying glass enabled me to see an insect with a new vision, the trout is hardly so equipped. We have some reason to believe that the trout's eyes do have a certain magnifying power, but if so it is at close range, and he usually sees first at greater distances the flies offered to him. It is at these distances that he will ordinarily decide whether or not the fly appeals to him. Therefore our flies should be constructed and colored so that his first impression is one of life and food.

A renewed appreciation of angling has resulted from the days spent on the stream in giving practical application to theories and clarifying the ideas set forth in this book. When one thinks as an angler and an artist at the same time, not only angling but nature as a whole is involved. This integration has given new meaning to my contacts with the stream and its surroundings.

The fact that angling is a contemplative recreation brings the angler a particularly acute consciousness of his surroundings. He is frequently alone on the stream. His conversation, if it can be called that, is with nature rather than individuals. He is made subtly aware of nature's reaction to his presence there.

Is there not a response to the angler as he responds to his environment? Do not the stream, the trees and the rocks react to his presence? Are they asleep? Or are they active, alive and offering a subtle contact?

The quality of such experience has great variety. Are we not all aware of the apparent changes from day to day in angling surroundings? There are days when the same river will seem to alter its disposition. It will appear more *alive* than ordinarily. The air takes on a charged quality, and we are at once conscious of a response which adds to our enjoyment and elation. The fishing is very apt to be better. We are keener, more alert and we expect a rise on every cast.

How often, too, one may feel the charged quality of one's surroundings, just before the rise of a fish. In that electric moment when everything holds its breath in expectancy, the very air seems to remain motionless. The water quiets itself so that the rise, when it comes, appears greatly magnified and even the size of the trout is affected by this quality of magnification and seems huge to one's excited eyes.

There are days, as well, when the deadness of the stream is only too apparent. On those days the line even floats badly. The water has no "feel." It grumbles its way along complainingly, rather than with joy in its movement. The consciousness of nature's response is a negative one; that electric quality is missing—and so are the rises. Those days are apt to be poor for fishing; the trout come with little enthusiasm, if at all.

One day I was on the stream with a friend, a writer, sensitive and observing, who had more than once called my attention to some rare quality in nature. When he entered the stream, he stood for a moment looking around him and then said,

"The water is lively today!"

Then he added, "This is my kind of fishing day and the trout will rise —you'll see."

At once I became aware of a peculiar *rapport* between us. Our awareness was close. Our reactions were similar and we fished that day with a concurrent enthusiasm. That was an interesting and memorable occasion for me, because it struck a response in my own feelings for nature.

Even in the earliest of my angling days, when I first put a line into water with the hope of "drawing out Leviathan," I believe there existed an awareness of this environmental contact. And I believe that I have always appreciated it.

It is fortunate for anglers that the trout is a wary animal. It is also fortunate that he lives in an environment conducive to his protection which, at the same time, affords to the angler in pursuit of him those surroundings which lend to the sport so much of its charm. "The contemplative man's recreation" is an apt phrase, describing well the quality of experience which so truly offers to angling one of its rare attributes.

Fly fishing in a stream is the epitome of all that is good in angling. The very water, in its never-ending variety, is a proper background for the elusive prize we seek to capture. And the trout is of like caliber, a clean, bright, colorful and lively thing which can hardly be surpassed in nature for sheer beauty. His sagacity is well remembered. His strength is deceiving, for he can constantly surprise us with his determination not to be brought to net. There is hardly a trout too small to afford some pleasure in the catching, and when one is so clever or so lucky as to outwit a big one, the thrill is augmented correspondingly.

In these pages, I shall make no attempt, in trying to advise some anglers less experienced than I, to cover subjects competently handled by my peers. I shall only touch upon them when necessary to add new developments or to augment their basic logic. I hope only to record a few observations, and if some angler may profit by them, it will add considerably to my pleasure in writing them. And I shall try to carry further some of the teachings of the good fisherman with whom I have been associated. If I appear to take for granted that the reader is familiar with certain basic points in angling, it is because I had rather have him become so through the works already accepted as standard.

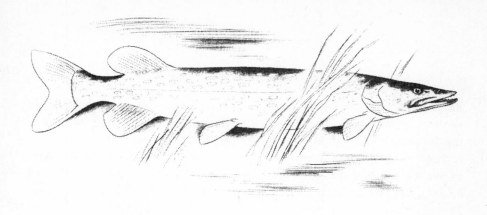

CHAPTER II *"Youth"*

IT SEEMED to me that my good fortune was almost overwhelming when I caught my first fish. As it happened, the fish was a good one, a great-headed pike that weighed four pounds and was almost as long as I. Such a sizable trophy was not only thrilling, but its bestial aspect—the big jaws filled with sharp teeth, and its long powerful body—was doubly exciting. It seemed to live for hours. I tried to dispatch it by various means but only succeeded after dragging it home and chopping its head completely off with the camp axe. Since that early day the expectancy and thrill of capture, whether of a trout, a lordly salmon or a six-inch bluegill, has lessened none in its intensity, and I hardly expect that it ever will.

Since then, the paths to the fishing waters have led to many interesting and wonderful places to cast a fly: the Washington rivers like the Spokane and the Little Spokane, the Satsop, Wynoochie and Humptulips (even the names are wonderful); the Cle-Elum, the Cedar, Deep Creek, and, in Oregon, the Deschutes, Crooked and Crescent Creek; in California the Pit, the Feather, the Merced and the Klamath; the charming streams of New England, the Catskills and Adirondacks—the Beaverkill, the Neversink, the Willowemoc, the Schoharie; the Ausable and the Battenkill. The mountain lakes in Idaho in the Coeur d'Alenes, the lakes in the Cascades of Washington and Oregon; the clear waters of the Sierras have all brought their own unique contributions. And the salmon rivers of New Brunswick and Cape Breton with their long gravel bars and dark spruces, the bright silvery fish up from the sea and the campfires on the river banks; the canoe on the brown waters of Maine, with the deer standing at the edge when we rounded a bend—these are all memorable and their remembrance brings lasting pleasures.

Angling has been responsible, to a great extent, for a life and a philosophy well suited to the temperament of the artist. It has taught me about art, as art has led to interesting theories and experiments in angling. Thinking and fishing go well together somehow. And the thinking is usually of the creative sort rather than the summing up of those difficulties with which we are all beset at times.

One of the great qualities of the sport is that it is non-competitive. Americans, in particular, seem to me well enough supplied with competition not to include fishing as well. The least flavor of the competitive destroys its most charming qualities, lending it an atmosphere of sly haste, pervading its associations with petty jealousies, envy and resentments. The angler who is determined to catch the biggest fish or the most of them, by his own determination becomes a competitor and is self-poisoned.

How wonderful to the fisherman is the anticipation of an angling excursion. The reality of experience often finds itself obliged to take second place to the pictures the mind can summon. In imagination, the angler is provided with unique sensations. In the fleeting moment he visualizes them, he enjoys emotions impossible to have been experienced in reality in such a short space of time. A whole day's happenings can be brought to the imagination in the twinkling of an eye. The mind can visualize the scenes frequented by the angler, with great beauty rarely found in actuality. The trees, filled with singing birds, are never in the way of his cast and are only placed there to afford him shade or shelter. The trout never come with difficulty, and he can make them in his mind's eye of a size in proportion to his enthusiasm.

I know a man who, due to ill health, is unable to go out on the river. He finds, instead, a great peace of mind and a great deal of enjoyment in taking what he calls a trip to a good trout stream. He will fish an entire river in imagination, working up from pool to pool, casting his flies to imaginary trout, raising some, leaving others unmolested and occasionally finding a good one which he confidently works over and takes with a masterly approach.

When one knows a trout stream after many years of having fished it, the experience of going back again, even by so remote a method as

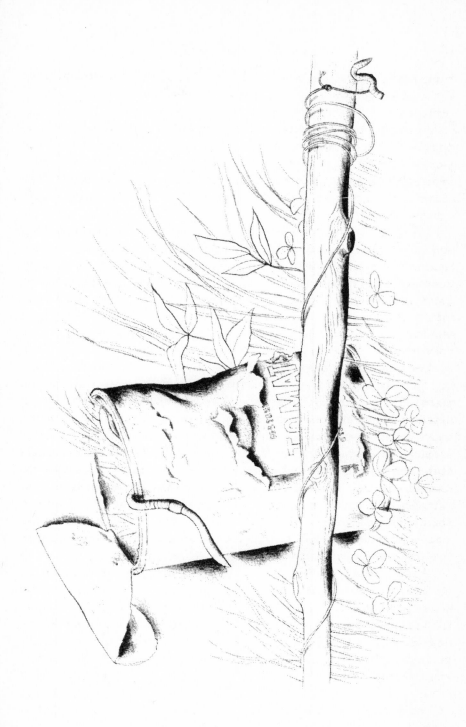

through spirit alone, can afford sóme delightful occasions. It is all gold and no dross.

In youth, of course, the angler does not need to rely on memory, imagination or those quiet hours of contemplation so pleasant after long experience. His is the active pursuit. He loves to explore new waters. He stalks his quarry with an enthusiasm and determination that rely more on strength and endurance than on guile. He may be prone to do a little poaching of the innocent sort, and his methods savor more of the hunter than the purist.

I remember well that my own youth brought few exceptions to these rules. Even though angling was beginning to be regarded more philosophically, and the beauties of the contemplative point of view finding roots in an active nature, I was apt to revert to impulsive and often unpredictable tactics. "Dapping" was one.

Did you ever "dap" for trout? If not, you have undoubtedly been deprived of one of the definitely exciting experiences of angling with the fly. Part of its fascination lies, no doubt, in the faint flavor of the poacher's art, the lack of which in any angler, particularly a young and intrepid one, is to be deplored rather than commended. It requires a certain stealth. It is flavored with an atmosphere typical of the small boy who creeps up to hook his quarry and fling it over his head with a shout of joy.

One year during my early angling wanderings, I spent a summer in Yosemite Valley, in California. The Merced River there, a lovely crystal-clear stream which hurls itself over great cliffs and rushes down between the boulders, flows out more calmly when it reaches the valley floor. There its banks become heavily overgrown in places, and there are sections where either it is impossible to enter the stream or one has no room to cast. There were places where the bushy cover extended out, over and even into the water, for several feet.

Naturally these difficult spots had trout in them. By cautious maneuvering one could peer down and see the heavy fish, secure in their environment.

The method I adopted to suit that occasion was hardly to be called the most pure, but it did produce some excellent results. I will only offer the apology that my tender years were responsible. I remember distinctly how delicious those trout tasted, due to their unusual method of capture I am sure!

Dapping, an ancient practice, is still used in Great Britain for catching trout during hatches of the large May flies. It usually consists of fastening the actual insect to the hook and allowing it just to touch the water where trout can be expected, not by casting, but by a mere lowering of the rod point, the angler being concealed, of course.

My own method was much simpler. I used a rather bushy dry fly, on heavy gut, and fished it on a short line, at most no longer than the rod. Only the fly touched the water.

At the time I visited that dramatically beautiful valley, the roads were scarcely more than sheep trails and we spent the entire day driving, up from San Francisco. There was a great deal less travel then than now, and consequently only a fraction of the number of tourists and anglers.

My quarters were in the old inn called Cedar Cottage, named from the enormous tree which grew right up through the building. It was only a stone's throw to the river and early each morning it was my habit to take a rod and try to catch a trout for breakfast. Along the bank there was a row of large trees, their roots making fine hides. One particular spot nearly always held a fish. If I caught him, another would appear a day or so later, and this favorite place furnished me with many a fine meal.

When I learned how to fish it properly, by the stealthy approach and the dapped fly, I could walk up carefully behind a big tree trunk, slowly push my rod around the tree and drop my fly without even seeing the water. Frequently I was only aware of the subsequent rise by hearing it, or by feeling the strong pull of the fish. It became almost automatic, this early morning execution, and you may be sure I was careful not to advertise my method. The trout in that particular spot varied little in size. They were exactly right to furnish a solid and substantial breakfast so I needed only one.

There were other good spots along the banks that also produced their trout at times. And there was considerable smashed gear, as often a heavy fish would be too much to handle in the tangle of branches and roots. Whenever possible I would haul the larger trout quickly up the bank, violently flopping. The small and medium sized ones could be levered out through the air as my rod was husky and my gear stout. With only the fly touching the water, heavier leaders could be used and they, of course, held many a fish that might otherwise have been lost. The fly patterns seemed to matter very little to the fish. It was the dapping that did the trick.

These daily expeditions brought me a certain reputation, and the cooks planned on the trout as an everyday article for my breakfast menu.

But if I failed to deliver I was badgered unmercifully, and it was with a certain loss of face that I was compelled to order a substitute.

One day I took a fish of about a pound in weight which seemed over-corpulent, and to find the cause, I opened him at once. The autopsy showed an animal entirely new to me. About the size of a mouse, but longer and more slender, with soft, mole-like fur and a flattened rudder-like tail, it was still in perfect preservation.

There was a natural history museum in Yosemite then, maintained by the Park Service, and I took my strange trophy over to see if they could identify it. The young man in charge was greatly surprised and remarked that only one other such specimen had ever been found there. It turned out to be a navigator shrew, and he begged it for his collection. The occasion led to a pleasant and long friendship.

There have been a lot of years and many casts since that memorable summer. My appetite for breakfast trout has diminished somewhat and an inherent laziness has increased considerably. With the conservatism of middle age, my angling has become more leisurely and, looking backward, it seems long ago that I last crawled up to a bank and hung my fly over an unsuspecting trout, ready to lever him out and hurry him home to the waiting skillet.

But there are still occasions when, standing out in the current and correctly casting my fly to the edge of the bushes, I have a recurrence of that early urge to more Indian-like tactics. Who knows, tomorrow it may get the best of me.

CHAPTER III *The Rise and "Light Pattern"*

THERE WILL always be differences of opinion among anglers regarding the rise of a trout in a stream, and rightly so; for as long as we do not know the reasons for his reactions to natural food and to our imitations, we shall have to be content with theory rather than fact. However, we do know what the trout sees, within a reasonable degree, and we can arrive at certain conclusions based on this knowledge which may help our fishing.

The laws of physics tell us that a fish can see *through* the surface of the water only within his "window"—a circular area on the surface which forms the base of an inverted cone, with the fish's eye at the apex. The included angle of the apex, ninety-seven degrees, is fixed and therefore the size of the fish's window varies with his depth in the water. Beyond the edges of the window, the surface of the water as viewed from below is a bright but opaque mirror; it reflects light but does not allow it to pass through. But anything outside the window which breaks or bends the surface of the water causes concentrations of light reflections in brilliant sparkling spots.

So when a fish sees a floating fly approaching, outside his window, he sees only the "light pattern" of sparkling dots created by each tiny part

13

of the fly that touches the surface. It may well be that the fish is able to identify various insects by their distinctive light patterns, particularly in a steady hatch, where identical light patterns closely follow one another. This may explain the reluctance of a steadily feeding fish to take a fly— natural or artificial—different from the one coming down.

As the fly continues to approach the fish, there comes the point at which, I believe, it is determined whether an exact imitation of the natural fly is needed to deceive the fish or a general approximation of it will suffice. It depends on whether the fish rises to the fly before it enters his window or waits for it to come in and gives it a close scrutiny before rising. If the former, the diameter of his window continually decreases as he moves upward, and if he has risen far enough ahead of the fly, it may remain beyond the edge of his ever-diminishing window until it is right over his nose; his mouth opens and he takes it automatically, before he has time to observe whether or not it is a fraud—or at least before he is able to inhibit his reflexive response.

We know, from the research of ichthyologists and anthropologists, certain facts pertaining to automatic reflexive feeding. It has been observed that the free-swimming fry of some fishes, when first out of the egg, begin a purely automatic opening and closing of the jaws. This occurs at nearly regular intervals, but is unconnected with breathing. Undoubtedly the gulping action of the tiny mouths results, at times, in the capture of some minute life forms which the fry swallows. This leads eventually to a directed effort and gradually the opening and closing of the mouth become reflexive only when food is visible.

Over periods of time these reflexes undoubtedly become fairly well fixed. Even though the fish is not hungry, the sight of food may be apt to cause a reaction before any inhibition takes place. I believe the automatic reflexive feeding habits to be responsible to some extent for the rise of the salmon to the fly. And there is good reason to believe that the steadily feeding trout depends less on a close scrutiny of the insect than he does on the light pattern which approaches him.

Of course the situation can be complicated by the effect of current speed and also whether or not the surface is ruffled. Whether the fly gets into the trout's window determines whether an exact imitation is needed. And the speed of the current and quality of its surface determine— to some extent—whether the fly reaches the window. If the current is moving fast enough, it will be almost impossible for the fish to ever see the approaching fly except by light pattern. He simply cannot get the fly in his window without turning and chasing it downstream. And he cannot afford to waste energy in taking such small bits of food as flies by turning downstream for each one and then swimming back.

On the other hand, when he tilts his body and moves forward, the pressure of the current on his under-surface helps to carry him upward, just as a ferry crosses a river on a cable or a boat sails against the wind. This force can scarcely be calculated but it is relatively considerable. Utilizing the same principle, most sailboats are faster into the wind than before it, and ice boats actually may thus sail far faster than the wind that drives them. It is only in a languid current and when a fish is full fed and finical, that one actually sees him turn and follow a fly or let the current carry him downstream beneath it. When the angler can see the fish, this is about as disconcerting as anything I know, particularly if the trout is a big one. This holding of the breath for what seems minutes before the fish makes his decision can do awful things to one's blood pressure. Naturally, these deliberate feeders require a fly which is a better imitation and will stand close scrutiny. The casting, as well, offers more difficulties. This type of rise and some methods of solving its difficulties will be discussed in the chapter on dry-fly fishing.

If my conclusions as to the reactions of trout to light pattern are correct, it would seem advisable to try and approximate the light pattern of the insect by the construction of our flies. Leaving the detailed impressionistic color theories until later, let us look at the means of achieving good light pattern.

This is governed entirely by the type of hackle and the manner of tying. It is easy to understand how soft and webby hackle would fail to suggest the insect properly; the entire fly would be in the surface film, creating an entirely different appearance from below. If one wishes to simulate, however, a spent spinner in the surface film, that is another matter. I am speaking now of the duns which furnish a much larger proportion of the trout's diet than the succeeding spinners. I believe that a great deal of the success of the variant is due to the fact that, when properly tied, it stands up on the points of its hackle and tail even better than the conventional artificial fly.

In the average dry fly, especially one tied for the trade, the hackle is apt to be bunched too closely. This makes a lovely neat fly and many anglers demand it, but the trouble is that its light pattern is unlike that of the natural. Also the bunched hackle tends more to break the surface

film. If the hackle were wound on with a lateral motion to spread it fore and aft, the light pattern it created on the surface would be more natural and besides the fly would ride better. A stiff tail, too, is an asset in keeping the fly high and the body off the water.

Lee Wulff achieves the notably natural light pattern of his flies by winding the hackle not only around the hook before and behind the wings but also criss-cross between the wings. This not only produces a wide spread of hackle on the water but lends the fly a rough, impressionistic silhouette, an important factor in the attractiveness of a fly apart from its light pattern.

The May flies have only six legs, and as a rule the tail does not touch the water when the fly is resting on its surface. Naturally we cannot expect to find hackle so stiff that six barbules would support the fly. But it is important that the fly be not overloaded with too much hackle. No doubt the effect to the fish when a dozen or two dozen hackle barbs touch the surface is one similar to that caused by a moving insect. There are more sparkling dots in the surface film. But the matted, drowned effect of poor hackle or too much hackle is entirely different, and has no resemblance whatsoever to the live dun.

It is obvious that to properly imitate the light pattern of a natural fly, the artificial should be of proper size. That is, the fly should create a proper sized light pattern. This could easily be governed more by the length and amount of hackle rather than by hook size; the use of a variant, for example, instead of a conventional pattern.

Here again, we are confronted by the problem which arises on slow, clear water, where the fish is a deliberate feeder. When the trout allows the fly to enter his window before rising, not only should light pattern be correct but silhouette, size and color as well.

As impressionistic color in flies is more apt to suggest life than solid tones, an impressionistic outline or silhouette suggests life more than a sharp outline. The trout sees the fly either against the sky (through his window) or under the surface of the water, in which latter case it is seen either against the shimmering under-surface or the stream bottom, depending on whether the fly is above or below the fish.

In any case, the fly should have a silhouette typical of the natural. The insect on the surface reflects light from both the sky and the water, as well as the bottom of the stream. This makes for a changeable, indistinct and soft outline which is further broken by frequent movements of the fly's legs and wings. The materials used in fly tying decide impressionistic form by their texture. Materials used for bodies should provide the soft outline suggestive of movement which only soft and translucent materials can give. There should never be a hard outline; even the wings appear more natural if they are broken up in silhouette.

Below the surface, the fly should provide reflection as well as translucence. The sparkle of tinsel may suggest the reflections of moving water on the color of the bottom as the fly travels on its course. And the soft filaments of the body dubbing may sometimes hold the miniature clinging air bubbles typical of the adult caddis fly which has re-entered the water to oviposit.

Hackle should add life to the silhouette when the wet fly moves in the current. Stiffer hackles should be used for the fly which is to be fished in fast riffles, while for flies to be used in slow or still water one should try to find hackles soft enough to appear alive with very little movement.

If the angler can adapt his flies and his presentation so that the effect on the trout is truly lifelike, he will have made a substantial advance in the right direction. If "the look of the fly on the water," as Theodore Gordon said, is right to him, the probabilities are that it will look better to the fish than if such were not the case. And if he studies the effect of his flies beneath the surface and arrives at a choice which contains these natural qualities, a great many of the difficulties of catching trout already have been surmounted.

CHAPTER IV *Wet-Fly and Nymph Fishing*

WHEN A FLY is cast on flowing water there are several factors that govern its movements. If it is a dry fly, it will float freely so long as there is no pull upon it of line or leader. When this pull begins, the fly starts to drag. It moves either across the current, down with the current at a greater speed than the flow itself or in a diagonal downstream direction. A fly beneath the surface acts in a similar manner.

When the pull of the line becomes strong enough or when the downstream course of the fly is arrested, it swings across the current below the angler. Then when line is retrieved the fly moves upstream.

These movements are the same whether the fly is a dry fly, a wet fly or a nymph. There is a slight variation, of course, due to the construction and weight of the fly, the speed of the current and the angler's position. But the course of the fly on or beneath the surface is very similar.

When a wet fly or nymph is allowed to drift with the current on a slack line, it tends to sink. Speed of current and weight of fly will determine how deep it will go. Then, when the pull of line and leader begins, the fly acts in a way similar to that of the dragged dry fly, except that it rises up from the bottom at an angle. As soon as the current exerts sufficient pressure on line and leader, the fly swings across current.

These movements of the fly can be varied, lengthened, slowed or speeded up by manipulation of rod and line. Extra slack can be fed through the line guides to attain a longer drift. Or the line can be "mended" to get the same effect. But the principle of fly movement—when drifting or being pulled by the line—is very much the same.

I have attempted to show, by this brief description of fly movements, that regardless of what type of fly one uses, one can only cause it to do certain things. If this conclusion is correct, I see no reason to differentiate between presentation of nymph or wet fly.

When we fish a fly beneath the surface we attempt to simulate the actions of natural insects. (Streamers, bucktails or any noninsect imitations will be left out of this discussion.) There are certain movements of nymphs and winged flies which are similar. All flies or nymphs drifting with the current, whether alive or dead, take a similar course. Nymphs and live winged insects both swim up from the bottom, against the current or across the current at every angle. As both natural nymph or winged fly act similarly, at least part of the time, there seems to be no reason to fish one imitation differently than another.

When trout are rising to the nymph or underwater fly, the angler should choose a fly as near as possible to the natural and fish it deliberately to the rise. He should hardly present his wet fly or nymph by dragging it across in front of the fish if the fish were taking nymphs drifting freely.

When we use the wet fly or nymph it is usually when no rising fish are visible. If there is a hatch, we put up a dry fly unless the trout are definitely nymphing. A great majority of the time we fish our sunk flies by covering likely water, hoping to find trout there. We are not attempting to imitate any particular natural fly. We use a favorite nymph or wet fly, one that is good under most conditions, and fish it in a variety of ways. If one method does not bring rises or strikes, we try another. This is how 90 percent of our wet-fly fishing is done.

In the following discussion of wet-fly and nymph presentation I will designate all sub-surface flies as wet flies in order to simplify the terminology. Bucktails and streamers are excluded.

Most of us are familiar with the rather rare type of wet-fly angler who seems to spend a great deal of time in one place, covering the water slowly and carefully and at times standing motionless and hanging his fly in a single spot. It seems to me that here we have a lesson in the use of the wet fly which we could all profitably practice. If the angler makes his presentation so that the fly comes slowly to the fish in his lie, requiring little, if any, effort on the fish's part to take it, and covers his water with the care of the dry-fly caster rather than the usual haphazard methods of the wet-fly man, the results will show him not only more fish but an increased pleasure in the sport.

Anglers are apt to look upon wet-fly fishing and dry-fly fishing as two entirely separated techniques. The wet fly is usually fished as a lure. The movements given it by the angler seldom are such that it appears to the trout as a natural food, acting in a natural manner. The orthodox wet-fly cast and manipulation of the fly places it in a separate category from that of the dry fly.

Unification of wet- and dry-fly techniques seems to be logical. Why should one, the moment he ties on a wet fly, ignore facts which govern his use of the dry fly? The sunk fly immediately takes on a new significance when we regard it simply as the presentation of an imitation of natural food at a different level. The only difference is that one is beneath the surface whereas the other is on top. And, of course, it is well known how much more of the trout's diet is obtained under the water than from the surface.

In the great quantity of material written about fishing the wet fly, little attention has been called to certain important factors of presentation. The admirable book on the greased-line technique for salmon which "Jock Scott" based on the fishing experiences and theories of Arthur Wood treats the subject very intelligently and its practice has done a great deal toward enlarging the scope of the low-water angler. But not many trout fishermen read books on salmon and I should like to mention some adaptations of the method to trout fishing, along with a few of my own theories concerning the presentation of the wet fly.

The usual wet-fly technique is pretty much a cut-and-dried affair. The angler casts his fly across, or across and downstream, and lets it swing around in the current, sometimes with movement imparted, sometimes "dead." In fishing with a tight line in this manner, the fly is apt to move too rapidly. For usually, after the cast is made, the pull of the current on the line and leader causes a downstream belly in the line. Then the fly is pulled downstream and whipped around in a manner resembling scarcely at all the action of underwater insect life. The fish often ignore such a presentation and the angler who always fishes his flies in this manner will frequently end his day empty-handed.

To bring the fly slowly to the fish is a different matter entirely and requires a different method. If the angler can control the speed of his fly by the cast and the subsequent manipulation of rod and line, he has already made possible a more lifelike presentation. Fishing in the manner of greased-line salmon fishing, the line is cast across current, or up and across, with enough slack to allow a free drift for some distance. This method has been described often but the reasons for its effectiveness have seldom been mentioned. It is not only the natural movement of the fly but the view of the fly by the fish that is greatly responsible for its success. For the fly is more apt to drift sideways in the current and the trout sees it from the side, where it is not only more noticeable but more attractive.

After the drift has been completed and the slack has been taken up, the line starts to pull the fly across the current. At this point, or before drag occurs, the line can be "mended." Mending means that a loop can be thrown either upstream or downstream, whichever way will allow the fly to drift on freely with little or no drag. If the fly is in slower water than the line, the line is mended by throwing a loop upstream. Contrariwise, if the fly is in faster water than the line, the loop is thrown downstream. These loops can be made by holding the rod well in front in a horizontal position. The line is then lifted from the water with the whole arm and rod as a unit, rather stiffly, picked up and rolled over to left or right. If slack line is held in the hand while making the mend, the extra line may be "shot" forward to form part of the loop. It is always a good idea to make the mend above the lie of the fish if possible so that any jerking of the fly—difficult to avoid, even in practice—will occur before the fly reaches it. By this mending, the length of the drift can be greatly augmented and the fly will be apt to remain in its cross-current position until it is almost directly below the rod.

The fact that the speed of the fly can thus be controlled is a great advantage and one never feels that it is shooting by the fish in such haste as to startle rather than attract. The fact that its drift is slightly across as well as down the current seems to make it no less attractive, and this delicate drag is probably even an asset. Once the angler understands the reasons for the effectiveness of this presentation, he can use any method to achieve similar results. It is very important that in all cases the fly should drift without the usual downstream loop in the line, as this immediately pulls the fly unnaturally, headfirst and rapidly downstream.

In the greased-line salmon technique, the line should float so as to facilitate mending and keep the fly near the surface where it is most effective. Due to the length of cast in most salmon fishing, a floating line is required to make these mends possible. The flies are small and lightly dressed for near-surface work. In these respects, the adaptation of similar methods for trout may be altered to suit requirements. The fly can be presented near the surface successfully for trout as well as for salmon.

Experienced anglers of a couple of generations ago who used the wet fly exclusively were very conscious of the theory of exact imitation. When trout were rising to a hatch of flies, they imitated the natural as best they could with their wet patterns and frequently cast and fished them as we do our dry flies. And, of course, they caught trout.

There are always a certain number of these hatching insects that fail to gain the surface. They are either drowned in freeing themselves from the nymphal shuck or are carried by the current down to the fish for some other reason. Theodore Gordon felt that the wet fly drifting down to a fish feeding on surface flies might be mistaken for the actual fly on the surface. I doubt this very much, as the appearance of the fly *in* the water is so completely different from that of the floating insect when viewed from below. Until the surface fly is directly over the fish, he sees it only as a light pattern and not as an actual fly, such as the drowned fly under the water. At any rate, we do know that wet flies fished near the surface are deadly at times, particularly when presented in a natural manner and not made to act more like a minnow than an insect.

The greased-line technique handles this situation admirably. Few of the thrills of dry-fly fishing are lost to it—the rise is nearly always seen and the whole process suggests more of surface than of wet- or sunk-fly fishing. However, when trout are not feeding on or near the surface and need to have the fly presented closer to their position, I prefer to fish by a similar method only with the fly well down in the water.

With the more deeply sunken fly and the slack-line drift or greased-line technique, it is useful to weight the body of the fly to make it settle well toward bottom before the pull of the line or leader starts it up through the water. I have never quite decided whether I prefer to grease the line for this deeper fishing but I am inclined to believe not. The ungreased line is more difficult to mend and by the same token less difficult to sink. If one uses as short a line as possible (a good rule for any fishing), it is not difficult to make the proper mends for a good drift.

Gordon was once questioned as to whether or not he greased his line for the dry fly and he discussed it at length. His final conclusion was that he generally preferred an ungreased line as it caused less trouble with surface shadows on the bottom. His conclusion was based on the effect on the fish rather than the ease or difficulty of working the fly.

When the sunken fly on slack line has reached bottom or near bottom

—which is where the trout spend most of their time—and the line first pulls on it, the fly suddenly becomes alive. It rises like an insect moving from its dwelling under a stone. I believe the moment at which the fly starts upward from the bottom to be the most effective in the wet-fly technique, not only for trout but for steelhead, Pacific salmon and many other game fish. It is simply a natural movement for a nymph or a fly which has emerged from the nymphal case and has started to swim to the surface.

It is fairly obvious that to present the fly properly to the lie of the fish is a more thorough as well as a more effective method than simply to cover the stream. And it can be easily understood how the angler might thus spend considerable time in one place.

If I find that fish do not take the fly on or near the surface, I usually make the cast more nearly upstream to allow the fly to get down in the water. By using plenty of slack and an occasional mend when necessary, one can allow the fly to drift a long distance before starting it up from the bottom. The point of starting the upward movement should, of course, be near to or at the spot where you expect to find the fish. With this slack-line drift one must be alert to recognize the rise or "take" of a fish, but I find that the fish frequently holds onto the fly long enough for the angler to feel him and set the hook. Usually, however, the fly is taken when it pauses and starts up from the bottom and at that point the fish is easily felt.

The main drawback to this method is that it takes many casts to cover the water. The angler should confine his efforts to the definitely fishy spots rather than try to cover the whole stream. In other words, simply fish wet where you would fish dry.

We are apt to neglect the wet fly when fish are rising, and when we find that they do not take the dry fly well, we blame it on the pattern. It is quite possible that wet-fly fishing and dry-fly fishing shade into one another on occasions, the dividing line being indiscernible. For instance, when the trout are taking small flies in the surface film not visible to us, we may be at a loss to solve the problem. A very thin, delicate wet fly, similar to those used by Mr. Hewitt in fishing the Neversink flats late in the evening, might be a good solution. I would suggest that in tying flies of this type the less dressing the better, within reason, as the trout get a very close look at the fly in the surface film or under the surface. This is particularly true in the evening when their vision is very acute.

Certain insects actually hatch under water and swim to the surface in the adult state and it is these that probably account for the success of flies with thin, sloping wings.

In using any wet fly which is to simulate the movements of the natural insect, it is possible to combine two or three types of presentation in a single cast. Use the slack-line cast, mend the line and fish the fly up from the bottom. Then, if in a fairly wide stretch of water, one can allow it to swing below at the finish to complete the cast more in the manner of the usual downstream technique. On the retrieve, allow the fly to drop back down a few times before it is picked up and recast.

To augment the drift of the wet fly, it is sometimes advisable to release slack line after the cast has been made, allowing the current to pull it through the guides, assisted if necessary by waving the rod back and forth. This method not only allows the fly to cover a greater area but also allows it to sink deeper. Water below the angler which may be too deep to wade or too far to reach by casting may be fished in this way and the method also eliminates any unnecessary movement by the angler.

Occasionally, the currents of a stream are such that none of the techniques I have mentioned would be practicable. For example, where an extremely fast current is directly in front of an eddy or stillwater. The slack-line cast is ineffective here, as the fly invariably would be swept out of the eddy and downstream. The best method of combating such a difficulty is to bring the fly across the eddy to the edge of the current, with a straight line and a high rod tip. The line is cast as straight as possible at an angle of about 45 degrees down- and across-stream. With the rod held high, allow only a small amount of line to lie over the fast currents—none whatever if possible. The swing of the fly is followed with the rod until the fly is below the angler. Actually the fly moves with fair speed—this can hardly be avoided; but it does move across current instead of down, and maintains a fairly even speed near the surface. It is important to start the fly out of the eddy before the current catches line or leader to jerk it abruptly downstream. The fly can then be fished across the faster water as it swings below. Trout that live in such eddies are well versed in taking their food from the edge of the current, and are quick to make a decision. They will come to the wet fly which is presented so that they are given sufficient time to take it. But we can hardly expect them to chase our flies downstream at express-train speed.

Using the straight line has one other advantage, not only in the situation that I have described but in more normal circumstances. That is, any touch of the fish is instantly felt, as the contact is direct from hand to fly. It also offers the disadvantage, typical of all straight-line casts and fishing, of having the fly lose a certain amount of mobility or freedom to follow currents in the water, due to the strong pull of line and leader upon it.

I believe that the speed at which the fly moves past the fish is the most important factor in its presentation. This may mean that in a very slow current the fly is not carried fast enough and speed must be added rather than subtracted. It is also essential that the pull of the fly be a steady one, with no full stops. Movement can be varied; small jerks used—but the fly is best shown the fish as a constantly moving object. When the angler can see the fish follow the fly, it can be very disconcerting if the fish hesitates in taking. But there should be no cessation of pull or the fish is very apt to be frightened.

If one strips in line with the left hand by simply pulling it through the guides until the hand is at a maximum distance from the rod, there is then a pause before the next stripping operation begins. It may be possible to keep the fly moving during this pause by raising the rod tip. However, I much prefer the hand twist retrieve method, which keeps the fly moving rather slowly but steadily. And small jerks may be added by the pressure, at intervals, of a finger on the line as it is retrieved. (This technique is discussed further in the chapter on salmon fishing.)

There is still another method of fishing the wet fly with which most of us are familiar. It has been described frequently in angling literature but is important enough to warrant mentioning again here. This is the technique where a dropper fly is used and in the retrieve is made to skip across the surface in the manner of a dapped insect. The rod and hand impart the motion. I personally seldom use more than one wet fly on the leader, but at times this particular method has a strong appeal to trout. It should be in every angler's repertoire. It is particularly useful when trying to move a stubborn fish by hanging the fly over him.

The method calls for the use of a short line, which is always an advantage and allows better control of the fly. One may try various methods of moving the rod, but I believe the most effective is one in which the angler shakes his rod hand as if he were affected by palsy. I once saw it described in those terms and, after trying it, was convinced not only that it was described accurately but that it worked better than any other movement I had tried. Ferrier Martin, an excellent wet-fly angler, uses this method with great success. He once took an incredible number of

trout from a spring-hole, about a hundred in one afternoon, by the "palsy" technique and dropper fly. That was on "Uncle Lloyd" Taylor's water in Warwick, N. Y. Of course the fish were not killed, but I never saw a better demonstration of how deadly the method could be.

We frequently run across anglers of prowess with the dry fly but it is really seldom that we see one who knows how to fish the wet fly thoroughly and effectively. I personally had rather fish dry whenever possible, as there is something particularly wonderful about the whole action taking place where I can see it. But actually the wet-fly technique offers infinitely more possibilities and can be a fascinating as well as rewarding way of taking trout.

Many of us are familiar with those exasperating days on a stream when we raise many fish but fail to hook them. As in other angling problems, there is hardly a clear-cut solution to a situation like this, but I believe that frequently when we blame the fish for our lack of success in hooking them, regarding it as something inevitable, we might profit by analyzing our presentation and trying to determine whether our poor luck might not be due to our own shortcomings.

The tentative plucks we feel frequently indicate a lack of resolution on the trout's part. He is unsure of whether the fly is what he wants and rises with hesitation, letting go of the fly at once. Or the cause might well be that the fly is moving too fast, causing the fish to strike short. When a trout or salmon really wants a fly, it is difficult to take it away from him, and one is sure, in feeling the solidity of the pull, that he is well hooked.

Not only can a change of fly pattern bring success but a change of direction of its movement, its depth in the water, its speed or the way it is retrieved can alter our luck as well. The fact that the fish came at all is proof that he is ready to feed. Then it is up to us to choose the right way of taking him. Once a trout is pricked by the hook he will probably not rise again for some time, but occasionally we will find him repeatedly plucking at the fly with obvious lack of fear. This will give us an opportunity to experiment on the same fish, which is an excellent way of finding a solution to our problem.

The most generally applicable rule for such conditions, if we can risk using the word "rule" in angling, is that there is something unnatural about the fly or its movements. It is much more apt to be the latter, too, than the former. Sometimes the size of the fly is important and the change to a smaller fly often brings the confident rise. More often, however, I believe the presentation itself to be at fault.

Change of position so that the fly comes to the fish from a new and different angle should help, particularly if the fish is accustomed to having other flies shown him from the same angle, day after day. He will at least be given the stimulus of variety. If we can get our fly deeper in the water and fish it more slowly, this will help overcome hesitancy on the trout's part. Frequently the light plucks we feel are only due to the rapid movement of the fly which does not give the fish sufficient time to make up his mind about it. He can't take it without expending too much effort.

I have spent many fascinating hours on the Neversink experimenting with the presentation of the wet fly and nymph and particularly trying to determine their effectiveness when fished up from the bottom.

In one large spring-hole with a lovely white sand bottom and such clear water that every action of the fish could be seen plainly were a host of fish of all sizes. I used to take a position slowly and carefully on the bank where the light was good and I could watch the fish. By moving cautiously I could cast a nymph over them. I tried several different types at various times but had little response to any except two or three very small ones—No. 16 or No. 18. The best were weighted so they would sink at once. Usually, as soon as the nymph entered the water and began to sink, a few small trout would swim up to it and look it over. In no case did a fish take it while it was sinking. I would allow it to reach bottom and leave it motionless for a time. Once a trout of 10 or 11 inches picked it up from the bottom and was hooked. With this exception those I actually hooked took the fly on its way up from the bottom. In order to induce them to strike at all, I had to move it very slowly and cautiously. Any quick jerks or abrupt movement seemed to frighten them. A slow retrieve, pausing to allow the nymph to settle slightly after each upward movement, was best.

There was another place in the Neversink where I could watch the fish and where I tried the nymph and wet fly in various ways. This was in a pool with a current of medium to slow speed and with a light-colored bottom where the trout could easily be seen. By slowly taking my position and remaining motionless until the trout became accustomed to seeing me there, I could quietly cast above them and let the nymph or wet fly drift down to them. If I imparted any movement to it other than a very delicate one, they showed fright at once. A few took when the fly was drifting freely but usually, as in the spring-hole, the moment when the fly started up from the bottom was the best.

In both this location and the spring-hole, a dry fly caused absolute consternation, the trout flying in every direction, no matter how carefully the cast was made, how fine the gut or how small or thinly dressed the flies. At other places in the river where the banks were well overhung with trees or bushes the dry fly was more apt to be taken, particularly spiders or variants. Considerable protection was afforded by the cover against natural enemies and the fish were accustomed to having a certain amount of food drop to them from the trees overhead. They were not apt to be so wild.

I am convinced that the wet fly is frequently a better fish-getter in low, clear and difficult water. In many instances the cast of the dry fly is itself enough to put fish down. With a wet fly which sinks well and a fine leader which does the same, the trout may be temporarily startled when the fly touches the water but seems to recover quickly when fly and leader sink and cast no magnified light reflections or shadows. The fly can be moved under the surface with no ill effects, if done with care, and frequently just the suggestion of a twitch is all that is needed to make the fish take it.

I believe that the angler who fishes slowly and thoroughly, not to say discriminately; who brings a more varied approach to his fishing and who suits his style to the requirements rather than to his personal preference for dry or wet, deep fly or shallow fly, will find renewed fascination in his sport. The seasoned angler who stands in one spot may appear to be missing a great deal to the man who hardly pauses in his passing. But I would wager that results will be decided less by the distance we cover than by the manner in which we cover it.

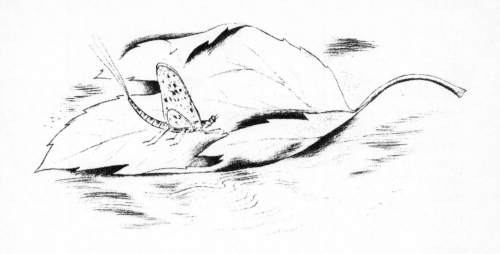

CHAPTER V *Dry-Fly Fishing*

THE SUBJECT of dry-fly fishing is apt to be more fully understood by anglers than that of the wet fly. The fact that the entire process is visible from finished cast to rise makes for less conjecture and more information about what happens.

Probably the most important part of the dry-fly angler's technique is his presentation of the fly. He may know the stream well, be familiar with lies of trout, but if he does not show the fish his fly properly he will go unrewarded. This does not necessarily mean he must be able to cast a long, "beautiful" line but it does mean that his casts must be effective.

Whether the angler is fishing dry or wet, *control of the fly* is all-important. When the methods of successful fishermen are analyzed, taking for granted that their streamcraft is equal, it is the angler whose fly is on the water the most and who is in control of it at all times that catches the most and largest fish. The more time wasted on faulty casts, the less chance there is for the fish to be risen. The long float is more effective than the short one, as the fly is being fished a greater proportion of the time. Any manipulations which can keep the fly longer in fishing position will increase the likelihood of contact with a fish.

The caster's position in the stream is all-important to a good delivery. It eliminates unnecessary length of line. It gives the angler other advantages in his cast which may have been lacking had he chosen a poor location. Of course, it is not always possible to stand in the perfect place from which to assail the fish, but with a little maneuvering it is seldom that one cannot improve his position.

For the right-handed caster, it is naturally better to be on the left-hand side, facing upstream. This allows more room for the back cast and makes the slack-line casts easier to execute. My ideal position is very nearly across the current from. the fish or where I think the fish should be. It is much easier to control the float and eliminate drag there than from directly below, the leader is not so apt to pass over the fish and, by keeping well to the side, I do not wade through productive water.

A large proportion of the casts made by the dry-fly fisherman are across a fast current to the far edge or into slow water beyond. This situation calls for some sort of slack-line cast to obtain a proper float. Naturally the fly should alight on the water downstream from the line and leader, or at the end of a series of curves in line and leader, so that the fly will not be jerked downstream soon after delivery. Many angling books contain descriptions of curve casts, so I will only suggest my own adaptation of standard methods. To make a curved cast to the right, I have found that a side motion, in fact a sort of underhand swing, is effective. Little force should be imparted to the rod, but rather a gentle, scooping movement with the rod tip finishing higher at the end than at the beginning. This causes the leader and fly to come down very lightly as the motion of the rod is stopped while the fly is still a foot or two above the surface. At the same time, the loop of line, being heavier, continues upstream or to one's left and falls above the fly. The right-hand curve can be increased by prematurely shooting a small amount of line. The upward swing of the rod causes considerable slack to fall when the cast is finished. If the current between angler and fly is very swift, I immediately pass the rod from right to left hand, holding the line upstream as far as I can. This adds considerably to the length of dragless float. It is even possible to mend the cast gently, directly after it touches the water, increasing the upstream loop. The fly should be allowed to float below the angler as far as the length of line will permit, or until a cross-current drag occurs. Actually, this slow drag is sometimes an effective way of raising fish, as I shall mention later.

If the angler, from necessity, has to cast from the right-hand bank, his problems are considerably greater. But even here he can improve his delivery and float with a little practice. If current conditions are similar to those already described—that is, with a fast flow between angler and objective—his loops or slack will need to be toward his right hand instead of his left.

There are two methods of achieving this result. The first is to use a similar scooping motion on the cast but at the finish impart considerable snap to the rod tip, driving the fly around in a curve to the left. The rod should be stopped abruptly and can even be pulled back slightly to encourage the curve. It is not necessary to pass the rod from right to left hand here, as it is already on the upstream side, but it can be held high and as far upstream as possible. A gentle mend is a help as well.

The other method is to make the cast with the rod held across the body and moving as it would if the angler were left-handed. This is sometimes essential if there are trees or bushes too close for a decent back cast on the right-hand side. If this method is used, the same movements first described are necessary—the slower, scooping cast and the movement of the rod immediately well upstream, but to the right.

When the stream is large enough or where the cast is of good distance, I would prefer a simple slack line delivery, from either side. This is best done nearly straight across-stream and by using more line than is necessary, stopping the rod high in the air and pulling back a bit on it to cause the loops to settle before the leader straightens out.

When casting in a wind, particularly a head-wind, it is often difficult to straighten out the leader at the finish. The fly is apt to light in a coil of gut. This can be overcome sometimes by a rather simple trick. As the line shoots forward, just before it straightens, stop it suddenly with the hand holding the line and jerk back on it, at the same time raising the rod tip. This motion tends to cause the leader and fly to continue forward and the fly will be more apt to alight properly. Naturally, this method should not be used if the angler wishes a slack-line cast. It is only to put the fly over a distant spot in a reasonably exact way.

The type of fly used has a great bearing on the cast necessary for proper presentation. As I fish with spiders and variants a great deal, I have had to develop certain special types of delivery. The air resistance is much greater, of course, and the forward drive of the rod needs to be more powerful than with the orthodox type of fly. In fact, it may be necessary to use a rod with more than ordinary power. In general, the cast must suit the air resistance of the fly, and with the small, lightly hackled flies the finish should be such that the fly never hits the water with force. The cast should be made so that its impetus is lost while the fly is still a foot or two above the surface; then it will alight naturally.

The spiders are wonderful for casting curves and slack, at least when the line is propelled faster or farther than the fly. But they are also a great handicap when trying to reach out a long distance in a wind!

What I have learned about fishing the spiders in movement has caused me frequently to wonder if anglers do not underrate the attractiveness of the moving fly of other types. There have been many occasions when a dragging fly, usually with a certain type of drag, has brought up fish which had refused the conventional float. It seems that the hardly perceptible drag is worst, and does not raise fish. But the deliberate cross-current pull is apt to cause them to take. With salmon, this method can be extremely deadly at times. It is possible that anglers, by adhering to orthodox techniques, are missing the good results of experiment. I will wager that in a generation from today (if, by then, there are any trout left to be caught), there will be many new ways of fishing the dry fly.

In the West, on some of the larger rivers, fishing is done mostly from boats. The angler casts downstream, stopping his rod and making a lot of slack to allow the fly to float down below him. Instead of picking up directly the float is finished, he retrieves his fly against the current in a series of jerks, sometimes on, frequently under the surface. As western trout are hardly to be classed as unsophisticated nowadays, it is possible that we Easterners are missing a good bet in not developing some of these methods.

The angler is frequently called upon to make a decision as to the "risability" of a trout. When he knows the fish is there, he should be able to judge whether or not it can be risen. If it has been frightened, he should know it. A great deal of time can be wasted over a non-riser, one which either is not on the feed at the time or has been put down without any visible sign that he has been frightened.

Frequently the trout may never change position from his regular lie when he begins feeding. If this lie combines protection and location in a food lane, it may be difficult to determine whether or not he can be risen. If frightened, he simply stops feeding without moving his position. Naturally, when the angler can observe the reactions of trout to his fly, he learns much. If the fish is near the surface, feeding on a hatch and for some reason stops rising and settles to the bottom, it is obvious that all is not well with him. It is also obvious that the angler had better leave him alone for a spell until feeding begins again or he has recovered from his alarm.

But when the reactions of the fish are not readily seen, there must be some point of time when a repeated presentation proves useless. I know some anglers who will stubbornly "stay with" a fish, casting and changing flies long beyond the point at which good results still could be expected. The angler of intelligence will decide when to leave the fish and try another, lest he waste effort beyond reason. At the same time, one should certainly not change his cast from one fish to another every time a new rise occurs. The fish being cast over may be just about to take, and should always be fished over for a reasonable length of time before moving to another.

When casting repeatedly to a single fish, one should try to achieve a sameness of float for a good number of casts before altering position or changing the type of presentation. The trout's very existence depends upon his judgment, and any fish worthy of effort has had ample opportunity to examine insects (and their imitations!) for some time. He must have confidence in his judgment and it may take twenty-five casts to bring that confidence to the point where he will accept the fly.

But if one obvious mistake has been made, the angler had better rest the fish for at least a few minutes before beginning again. If the fish can connect the appearance of the fly with something he does not like, one can hardly expect him to rise until that experience has been forgotten. Unfortunately, the fish is not a reasoning animal and appears, as well, eccentric and moody in the extreme. The result is that a great deal of theorizing can only be based on isolated experiences. But from years of trial and error come certain reasonable assumptions, and at least these afford us a basis from which to work.

We know that certain occurrences when repeated for some time cause trout to accept them without alarm. For example, everyone knows how seldom it is that fish are affected by people swimming in a pool, or by the presence of wading cattle. True, the fish usually move away, but frequently they can be seen rising unconcernedly near by. But after one experience with a cow which resulted in severe alarm, it would be some time before they would accept that cow as a harmless neighbor.

One of my friends claims that his best bass have been taken near the floats used by swimmers. Frequently he has cast to the edge of a float and hooked good fish at the same time that swimming was going on. Bass are not trout, of course, but frequently they react similarly. The fact that no swimmer had ever caused them more than a momentary inconvenience apparently was enough to encourage a feeling of safety under those conditions.

I have stood within a rod's length of large trout or salmon where they could see me perfectly. But I attained that position very slowly and carefully and made no sudden movements. We can hardly expect the trout to connect the arrival of the fly over his head with the dimly seen pair of waders and the slowly waving rod. He must feel that since those objects show no visible tendency to cause him hurt, he can go about his business unconcerned. But he will undoubtedly keep a weather eye cocked in that direction and any sudden movement or alarming shadow will send him quickly to cover.

The angler should be aware of such basic animal reactions and conduct himself accordingly. When he does not understand how his fishing will affect a trout, he should at least be circumspect. He should apply his knowledge, his experience and the resulting judgment *before* he casts his fly, and not wait until he sees that the fish has gone down. For example, when I described the deliberate riser, the trout that is prone to back slowly down under the fly, examining it minutely, I spoke of one of the truly fascinating problems facing the dry-fly fisherman. If the trout has been taking natural flies in the same way, the rise that we see is well below his actual lie or position. Casting to the rise would hardly raise him—he would be several feet upstream. One must either know the habits of fish in a particular lie or watch sufficiently to be able to tell where the trout's real position is, and cast accordingly. This type of rising fish necessitates a very long, dragless float too, as a rule, and makes the whole presentation more difficult. It is certainly important to allow the fly to float well below where we think the fish is before picking up, or we may frighten him.

I frequently employ the following type of presentation to a fish I am not sure of: I cast well to his near side and possibly a bit below him at first, gradually extending the cast until his exact lie, or where I believe it to be, is covered. By keeping the fly to one side he is less apt to be frightened, and sometimes he will come to it even if it is still short of his position. It is much less risky then throwing over his feeding lane, where if he is higher up than one imagines, one may spoil things.

My friend and fellow-illustrator, Mead Schaeffer, uses this system a great deal but partly for a different reason. If he knows approximately where a fish is lying, and especially if he is fishing a big spider, he will work each cast a little nearer the fish, from the side. When finally the fly is directly over the fish, it is very apt to be taken as the fish has been aware of it, becoming more excited as he sees it draw nearer. Mead swears by this treatment, and as I have seen him lure some very hefty trout to their doom, I believe its effectiveness is not overestimated.

When fishing banks or along any obstruction, it is good to remember that if the trout is actually underneath something, he cannot see the fly if it is cast very close. Therefore it is better to approach the hide gradually with successive casts so that the trout can see the fly as it approaches. He may become interested and move out enough to enable the angler to cast directly over him. Sometimes, of course, it is necessary to get the fly very close to the bank, log or whatever forms the edge of the flow, and I have frequently found that even a couple of inches will make a difference. The big spiders are excellent for this type of fishing, as they can be cast directly onto the bank or log and twitched off into the water. They rarely become hooked as the long, stiff hackles prevent it. When a cautious trout sees something that looks edible quietly drop to the surface from the bank, he is usually convinced that Nature has arranged it that way and has no suspicions.

Where there is a rock, log or other obstruction lying across the current, the situation can offer interesting possibilities. The upstream side of the obstruction will be a collecting point for food and the trout is apt to choose that particular spot for his feeding position. He may even take up his permanent abode there if other conditions are suitable.

The angler often passes up these places as too difficult. Actually, in many cases, a fly can be cast to such a spot with little danger of becoming hooked up if the angler will only study the flow of the current and choose a proper position. If possible, one should stand across from and a little above the obstruction, placing the cast sufficiently upstream so as not to "line" the fish.

In current of slow or medium speed, you will notice that there is a slight curl to the surface as it turns to follow around the upstream edge of the obstruction. Actually, the surface film or "skin" of the water—which is what supports the fly—is elastic and bends with the surface. When the fly floats down to this curl, it will usually turn and follow the edge of the obstruction to where the current flows around the end unless it is dragged under by line or leader. This would hardly be true in heavy, fast or rough water. There the force of the current would throw the fly up and around or as quickly suck it under the log.

When the cast is made, the line and leader must not pull from below. It should be thrown so that the fly is farther downstream than the leader and line, to give the fly time to turn in the current before it is dragged

downstream. The end of a log is a fine position for a fish, as here the most advantageous collecting point for drifting food is located. But I have frequently found that trout will lie along the entire upstream edge of the log, under it sufficiently for protection but in position to watch the edge of the flow.

Naturally the angler can expect the hooked fish to dart under the log immediately after rising, and many are the broken leaders and lost fish resulting. But these conditions are always attractive from their element of risk, and it would be a timid angler indeed who was too fearful of the consequences to hazard such an opportunity.

I remember once having considerable success in tackling a similar situation. It was in the Swamp River, a slow, deep stream that flows north into the Ten Mile River in lower New York State. I had left the stream after a long and not particularly productive day, at least in trout taken, and was walking back to my car along the railroad track which parallels the stream. As I passed, like all anglers I cast an occasional look over the water in hopes that there would be signs of rising fish.

The stream made a long bend, and glancing down its course to the west where the fading light made a bright band of reflection, I saw the widening ring that denotes a feeding trout. It was enough to cause me to scramble hastily down the railroad embankment and up the stream, enthusiasm once more aroused. When near enough to look over the situation closely, I discovered four trout in position along the upstream side of a big log which stretched nearly across the stream.

It was a tricky-looking proposition at best, and for some time I was undecided as to just how to present the fly. Then, by watching the flow, I could see that whatever floated on the surface down to the log was directed along its edge as it hit the little curl in the current. It took careful maneuvering, as I had to be a little above the fish, but they continued to rise. I had on a Fanwing Royal Coachman and made the first cast to the fish nearest me and nearest the end of the log. The current brought the fly down to the little curl. It bobbled a bit and then began to drift along the edge as if following a channel. I kept the line from pulling under, and as the fly reached the end of the log the trout took it.

I ended by taking all four fish, and it made one of the really memorable occasions to look back upon. The trout were of good size too, the largest being a good fifteen inches and the smallest about twelve. I had to wait for some time after taking the third fish, as he was quite close to Number Four, but the last one finally began rising again and I took him as well, all on the same fly. They were heavy, fat, wild brook trout, and I remember they made very good eating, too!

The mechanics of the rise in a situation such as I have described are apt to be somewhat different than the usual rise in open water. The trout will probably lie under the log in a position to see what approaches him on the surface as well as beneath the surface. He will be conscious of the light pattern of the fly before it reaches the curl on the edge of the current. But as he usually waits for the fly to reach the curl and start its drift along the log, he undoubtedly has opportunity to observe it more closely through his window than the trout who rises to pure light pattern.

For this reason, the whole situation is more delicately interesting, and the fly should be one which approximates the insect being taken as closely as possible, either by silhouette or color, or both.

In the experience I have described, where brook trout were the fish, the sure-fire Fanwing Royal Coachman was a good choice, but a rising brown trout is another matter. This does not necessarily mean that it would not take the Fanwing, as we all know what a killing fly it is on all kinds of trout. But I would imagine that when a feeding brown trout is encountered, it would be good policy to use a fly which appears approximately like the natural. If he refuses such a fly, it is then good practice to alter the pattern to one entirely different in size, form and color, such as the Fanwing.

Many anglers ignore shallow water for trout, particularly for brown trout, but anglers of experience know how frequently they can be found in water which is surprisingly thin. It takes a slow, careful approach to stalk fish under conditions where the water is still, but often in the fast riffles they can be cast to more confidently, due to the lack of visibility in the broken current. There are certain fast shallows in my favorite river which continue to amaze me by the size of the trout they produce, particularly along the banks.

During the warm weather, it is a habit of mine to fish often a stretch of water of this type. By four o'clock in the afternoon the best side of the river is in shade, and in the well-aerated water the trout seem to rise readily when the other stretches are unproductive. The trees extend out over the stream and it is pleasant fishing to move slowly along, each little pocket a potential trout producer. I cast my fly between the edge of the shade and the bank, covering all likely spots. The trout are usually in the shallow coves along the bank where an indentation causes a slight slowing of the current or a little stillwater. Sometimes the depth is no more than a few inches and the rise seems almost alarming in proportion, out of all scale with its environment.

One day a few years ago, Mead Schaeffer and I met one afternoon on the stream, and immediately each began to relate to the other how he had found wonderful sport along those shallow edges. I doubt whether either of us listened too politely for we each had so much to tell and a great eagerness to tell it. It was a coincidence that we had both decided to try similar water that day when the good fish came so readily, and many and long were the anecdotes.

When trout come poorly in the pools and flats, or when the bright sun or high temperature slows the fishing, the tree-hung riffles where the flow pauses by the banks should be one of the knowing angler's most rewarding objectives.

CHAPTER VI *Cold Weather . . . Streamers and Bucktails*

SOME ANGLERS on our Eastern streams are convinced that most of the good hatches occur on warm days, and that the usual hour for the emergence of the duns is late afternoon or evening. Of course we do have hatches at those times, but certainly not throughout the season. In early spring some of the most important appearances of May flies have been on cold, gray days when one would hardly expect the little duns to have the courage to emerge. Until well into May, the hatches ordinarily appear between ten o'clock in the morning and five o'clock in the afternoon.

A great many anglers instinctively prefer the late afternoon and evening fishing. This might be a good choice in August but earlier in the year it would not abide with my experience. Until about June fifteenth I would certainly choose the middle hours of the day as being the most productive. Unless the weather were unusually hot and dry, I would expect to find more activity on the stream then. Several important hatches in late April and early May appear at one or one-thirty o'clock and some begin at about eleven o'clock. There are apt to be flies on the water at any time between ten and three o'clock, possibly not in great numbers but enough to cause trout to feed. This kind of day can produce excellent results. With only an occasional fly coming to the fish, he is less apt to be selective and the angler can more readily get him up to a fly other than the exact imitation. It makes for more relaxed fishing than during some of the heavy hatches, when the atmosphere is apt to be frantic and wearing.

After the weather warms up in late June, July and August, the evening emergences of flies are the usual thing. Evening temperatures are lower then and trout are apt to feed more than during a hot, clear day. However, a great many evenings will find no real hatches of duns but only a few caddis or stoneflies and the inevitable and irritating midges. The angler will be more apt to find the fish in a taking mood if he is sufficiently active and ambitious to rise very early in the morning. Water temperatures usually continue to drop—or at least remain lower—until the sun appears and starts them up again. But at that hour most of us are enjoying a much less active pursuit than angling, and I am afraid that the added attraction of more and better trout will hardly compensate for those last few hours of sleep. I can remember that when I was a great deal younger and more eager to fill my basket, there were quite a few occasions when those early hours paid off extremely well.

In the early spring days when the water and air are both cold, the fish are apt to be sluggish in their feeding. But I can remember one particular hatch when the trout were unusually active. It was on the Kinderhook, and during several days of weather so dark and frigid that we were obliged to adopt clothing more typical of the ducking season, we took only a few trout of any importance, and those on wet flies. Once for about an hour at noontime, the fish came well to a wet Quill Gordon. One of our party had fished a stretch downstream, ran into a fine hatch and returned with some good trout. We had seen no flies where we fished, so the next day we went down to where he had found such good sport. At about noon I began to take fish on the wet Quill Gordon and after an hour or so a few duns appeared. The fish began to rise and I changed to the dry fly. For the next two hours it was almost unbelievable how many trout, and good ones, showed where nothing had even been suspected before.

I alternated between a Quill Gordon and a similar pattern with a translucent cellophane body—both were effective, I only needed to locate a fish of the proper size and cast to him; we could pass up the small fry and walk along the stream until we saw a rise denoting more desirable proportions. The trout almost invariably came to the fly and our only trouble was due to our excitement and haste, which spoiled an opportunity now and then. The low temperature on that occasion certainly seemed unpropitious for the dry fly, but the results were about as good as any I ever saw.

In Idaho, where the trout season used to be open during the winter months, I found that the little native cutthroat would take a fly readily, even a dry fly. It was mountain country, in the Coeur d'Alenes, and there was six feet of snow on the ground. I used to fish a medium-sized brook there on the days when the weather permitted, and it was my first (and last) experience of casting for trout from a snowbank. After a thaw or two had settled the snow sufficiently to allow travel without snowshoes we would hike upstream two or three miles above the little town and try our luck. The trout rose well to a small black-hackled fly and were delicious eating. There were no worries about preserving them properly; we simply laid them out on the snow until we were ready to leave.

The heavy crust covered the small spruces and it was weak where the tops were hidden just under the surface. We frequently crashed through, and the resulting battle for equilibrium was complicated by the stiff and prickly branches. Over our heads in deep snow, clutching our rods, we floundered mightily to regain footing. As I remember it vividly, no rods were broken, but our vocabularies were incapable, at that time, of clearly expressing our feelings.

When the trout season opens and the angler is filled with impatience to be on the stream again, he frequently encounters conditions which are hardly propitious for fly fishing. Rather than stay at home and wait for warmer days and lower water, he is apt to try his luck with a bucktail, a streamer or big wet flies. Trout are logy, then, and lie deep in the water. The lure needs to approach them closely to excite their interest and the angler is likely to need a weighted fly or some other method of getting the fly down to them. Too, later on in the season, during high water or when cold weather causes a spell of inactivity, again the big flies may turn the trick.

Most anglers will agree that warm-weather fishing is more enjoyable, but going fishing is what is important and if it necessitates cruder methods, that is better than nothing. The chance of raising a big fish is more likely during high or cloudy water; they seem to lose a certain amount of their caution then, and are more apt to take a well-presented fly.

To regard the minnow-like bucktails and streamers as only good in high water is a great mistake, for the proper type sometimes produces surprising results in low water. Tiny streamers, for example, tied very thin and light on a No. 10 or 12 hook, may be fished on 3x gut. With the added mobility permitted by the finer leader they have an irresistible motion in the water. They are excellent for pocket water and fast riffles, where the fly can be fished near the top. They even can be cast upstream, or nearly so, and worked down and across with small jerks. Changing currents alone

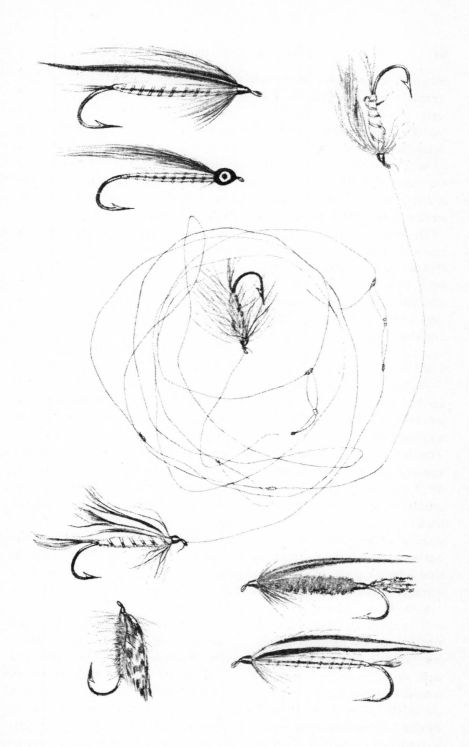

will give surprising life to a small fly like this on fine gut. They are very simple to tie. I usually use a silver body and a pair of small hackles of various colors tied over the back. No body or shoulder hackle is needed; for the wings ginger, badger and some of the crossbreeds such as cree are good.

In former years I used to spend considerable time on the Housatonic in Connecticut. Below New Milford it is a very large river, and formidable wading in places. There was one location there that, at times, produced some beautiful fishing for rainbow trout. We had to wade to the middle of the stream on a long bar and follow it down for three or four hundred yards to where the river deepened and wading was no longer possible. There was deep water on either side and two of us would fish it with these little streamers or very small bucktails. The fish took the fly almost directly downstream, and as we could not follow them, we could only hang on and hope for the best. Many broke off but a considerable number were landed—fine, heavy fish of extraordinary power. The most successful bucktail there was a simple little fly with a silver body and black or brown hair over white, tied on a No. 10 hook.

Probably the best bucktail for early-season fishing that I have ever used is the dark Edson Tiger—the one with a yellow chenille body and a brown bucktail wing. This fly has held up surprisingly well every season and I would never be without some. I usually weight a proportion of those I tie, for occasions when it is necessary to fish the fly well down in the water. Lead fuse wire is best for this, but the fly should not be made too heavy for decent casting. The old brown-and-white or black-and-white combinations always perform well, and I usually include a few streamer patterns made with wings of grizzly hackle, which is good for rainbows, along with the standard patterns of Black Ghost and Gray Ghost. The Black Ghost seems to be more effective when marabou feathers are used for wings in place of the white hackles. The softness of the marabou feathers gives an unusually fine action in the water.

Here again, as with dry flies, the opportunities for the fly tier to create new patterns are excellent. There is hardly an end to the combinations which achieve a minnow-like appearance and action in the water. Whenever possible, the local forage fishes should be studied and copied. While in the West recently, I ran across a pattern which killed well for me on several varieties of trout. It is called the Spruce Fly, and although I do not know who designed it, or whether it is based on anything in nature, I will vouch for its effectiveness. The dressing follows:

TAIL	three or four strands of peacock sword herl
BUTT	red wool or silk
BODY	peacock herl
HACKLE	badger, rather long and soft
WINGS	two badger hackles about one and one-half times the length of the hook shank. In case the regulation length hook is used, make the wings about twice as long. The wings should be tied back to back, making a decided V over the body. They should not project above the body much, but should be nearly parallel with the hook shank.

When fished, the opening and closing of the spread wings gives life to the fly. It should be allowed to pause in the retrieve to permit the hackles to open and be jerked slowly to close them again.

As a matter of fact, this type of wing well could be employed on other streamer patterns to add considerably to their lifelike appearance in the water. It is always well to remember that the softer, more mobile hair and feathers are better than the stiffer types; there are many varieties of hair now obtainable which are excellent. Their sheen and translucence in the water are also an advantage.

In fishing streamers, it is important to handle them slowly enough so that the trout has sufficient time to look them over. They should create, by their movements, as natural an effect as possible. When the fly is fished near the bottom it is sometimes necessary to cast obliquely upstream rather than across or down. The same arguments hold true here as in any other underwater presentation. It is the fly that moves up from the bottom which is deadly. There are occasions, of course, when the fish seem to like a fly moved rapidly near the surface but these are apt to be in the minority. Don't ignore the attractiveness of the bucktail when dry and floating, even though this may seem like a queer method of raising trout. Several times I have missed a fine, smashing rise to a dry bucktail, simply because I was unprepared. The fly had been cast out dry and was being moved across the top of the water, its outspread hairs looking like nothing under the sun.

In the West, due to the prevalence of very large stoneflies and caddis, it is common to use a big heavily hackled dry fly with large deer hair wings tied almost like a bucktail. These flies are frequently fished by jerking them erratically along over the surface, and in this manner some fine trout are bagged. It is unfortunate for Easterners that such hatches of big flies do not occur here. The quantity and size of these insects is almost unbelievable, some of the stoneflies being as much as two inches long.

I can remember, when a boy in eastern Washington, seeing tree trunks and stones near the water completely covered with them, while every large trout in the river seemed to be feeding. On the Pit River in California I once saw a hatch of caddis: trout of four or five pounds could be seen breaking, even leaving the water completely for the big flies. At that time we had our best success with a fly called a Light Caddis, fished just under the surface. It was tied on a No. 6 or 8 hook with a pinkish orange body, wings of mallard side feathers and light red-brown hackle wrapped palmer-style. Many were the smashed outfits when the big trout would head downstream through the heavy water.

Some rivers seem to hold many more forage fish than others and this fosters minnow-feeding by the trout. I frequently used to see large trout chasing minnows in the shallows of the East Branch of the Delaware, once a wonderful river for big browns. It is surprising how these large trout will occasionally do their feeding in the middle of a bright day; it makes catching them an extremely difficult proposition. Once, at the tail of a long flat, a sudden commotion in the water against the far bank drew my attention. As I looked, three very large fish swam out and began cruising around in the open. Several times, one would dart up into the shallows, leaving a huge wake and wallowing half out of water. As quickly as my nervous fingers would permit I put on a streamer fly and, without moving closer, cast above them as softly as I could. As I retrieved the fly I saw a long, dark shadow turn toward it, and held my breath in expectation. There was little current and the fly swung very slowly so I had to keep it moving by the retrieve. The trout suddenly made a vicious dash at the fly, but without touching it. I was in a quandary, as I felt I should not stop the retrieve even though I was afraid that if I brought the fly any closer he would see me. I had to do something, however, so I slowly brought it on through the water. Several times the big trout made sudden darts and swings, mouth open as if to take it, but in each case failed to connect. Finally he was near enough for me to see the color of his eyes and count his spots. When the fly was only about a rod's length away and had swung so that the trout was looking squarely up at me, he decided things were not as they should be and with a surge of his big tail that left a wake like a salmon's shouldered off across the pool. That was the end of that, as none of the three showed again. There was evidently something.

about the fly and its action that the big trout didn't like. I am afraid I never did decide exactly what was wrong. The clear, bright day and the shallow water were, of course, no help.

The river that I fish the most has few forage fishes. This results in better fly fishing, the trout being more disposed to be insect feeders. But, in other streams, we are frequently obliged to use the minnow-like lures to bring up fish. If one is at all observant, it is not difficult to locate the trout which are chasing minnows, as they seem to be unaware of the commotion they cause; at least they ignore it. If this takes place in the evening, they can often be risen to an imitation. It requires a cautious delivery, for the shallow water makes them very conscious of any disturbances and they are always more on the *qui vive* there. The thin, lightly dressed streamers are more effective under these conditions, as they can be cast with a minimum of fuss and sink quickly and easily.

Brook trout are very apt to be "suckers" for a bucktail or streamer, particularly a fly such as the old and trusty Mickey Finn. It is sometimes almost murderous to use these flies when the fish are in a taking mood, as it seems that one may catch an entire school of trout before they realize what is happening. Brook trout are apt to school together this way, not only in ponds but in rivers as well. The unscrupulous angler who happens onto such a congregation when they are hungry is apt to make serious inroads on our trout supply. This is one of the reasons why I believe brown trout are so much better game than brook trout; I have never found them so easily caught. It seems to me that the introduction of these fish has infinitely improved the sport, although we all love the native and his lovely coloration. There is no fresh-water fish that will compare with a wildwoods brook trout in courting dress, fresh from the water, with his vermilion spots surrounded by the little blue halos, the olive vermiculations on his back and the orange and scarlet of his sides, belly and fins. But he is an inferior breed when it comes to self-preservation and can hardly hold his own against the modern angler.

The large flies, bucktails and streamers can be used to great advantage in locating big fish. Sometimes the angler, in covering a bank where there are good hides for trout, raises one which comes short or only shows himself for a moment. These fish can be tried for with smaller flies once the angler knows where they are. Frequently the big spiders, or skaters, will take them. It is hardly feasible to cast repeatedly to a fish with a bucktail, but a small fly or a spider can be presented a great many times, if done with care and by resting the fish, without ill effects. It sometimes requires a fly as meaty as a bucktail to induce a well-fed trout under a root or in some other good spot to show himself, after which he often will succumb to another lure if he is worked on intelligently.

Most anglers will agree that big trout are apt to prefer big flies. They evidently feel that it is a mouthful worth trying for. Looking backward through the years, I can recall how well the large flies have served me in catching big trout, particularly in the West where the great, wild rivers grow such fine specimens. The Feather River in California was one of the best, and my first trip there to try out its rushing currents and heavy rainbow trout is well remembered.

When I dropped off the train at the little station early one morning I had my first look at what was, at that time, one of the State's outstanding trout streams. There was nothing more in sight when I climbed down from the sleeper than a little shed, a water tank and a solitary individual standing on the cinder platform.

It took but a moment to determine that this man was my host and, after shouldering my duffel bag, we struck back along the right of way to his little hostel on a high bank over the river. My first questions, of course, were about the fishing, and by the time we arrived and I had been shown to my quarters I had listened to a series of tales which greatly increased my already keen desire to try my luck.

The tackle was unpacked and my host was particularly interested in the flies I had brought. It was in midsummer and my selection had been tempered by the weather and height of water in the coastal streams near San Francisco. The result was that my boxes were filled with small flies. I had a very light rod, and fine leaders as well. He looked closely at my tackle, which he pronounced much too light for the river, and my flies, which he dismissed with a glance as too small for a decent fish. Reaching into his trousers pocket, he pulled out a mass of stuff resembling grocer's twine, tangled up with two or three disheveled objects which looked like dead sparrows. These I made out, after examination, to be leaders with wet flies attached. The flies were huge things, 4s and 2s, and the gut substantial, to say the least. How he avoided major injuries with those husky barbs so close to his anatomy I will never know.

The first rise I saw in that stream, if it could be called a rise, was a tremendous wallowing splash across the pool; I looked up in time to see the tail of a trout of unbelievable proportions disappear into the white water. My host above me on the bank said,

"Did you see that?"

I replied that I had indeed—how could I possibly avoid seeing and hearing a commotion of such magnitude? And I added,

"Have you any of those large flies to spare?"

He said, "That was Bill out there; he's been there for I don't know how many years. Nobody can catch him. He'll go about fourteen or fifteen pounds. Sure you can have some flies, but I wish you wouldn't catch Bill. I like Bill and I like to see him once in a while."

I didn't catch Bill nor did I hook him but while trying to, in spite of the wishes of my host and when he was well out of sight, I hooked a very solid, heavy fish that for a moment had me convinced that he *was* Bill. He proved to weigh an ounce under four pounds and was my best fish of the trip. The current was unbelievably strong, with huge boulders and plenty of white water, and the trout was out and around a great deal before he gave up. He took a big wet fly on a No. 4 hook, a real mouthful, more like a salmon fly than what I had been accustomed to fasten to my fine leaders.

The little rod held up well enough until later that evening. I had taken a good string of those big rainbows, all on the large flies, and was about to call it a day when I had a very heavy strike. The slow, ponderous movements of the fish and his powerful surges, unaffected, it seemed, by my pressure, convinced me that I surely had fastened either to Bill or one of his immediate family. After about ten minutes of battling this Leviathan in the heavy current I managed to lead him into quieter water. There I had my first look at him. When I saw that my fish was not Bill or even a rainbow trout but a tremendous squaw-fish, my chagrin was complete. The squaw-fish, like the Eastern chub or, as Sparse dubs it, "Beaverkill Tarpon," is as heartily disliked in the West as it is on the Beaverkill. One difference is that the squaw-fish reaches much greater weights. When this ugly, thick creature was discovered as the cause of all the excitement, I was so incensed that I gave a great heave on the little rod, which broke cleanly off at the butt.

The fish was eventually beached, as he had swallowed the fly completely and the heavy leader held him. It was either get him off somehow, break in him or spend the night in the river, and I was just mad enough to want to get my hands on him. His weight will never be known accurately as I threw him as far as I could in a general northerly direction. It was like putting the shot, only much slipperier. And if I remember rightly, not much lighter in weight.

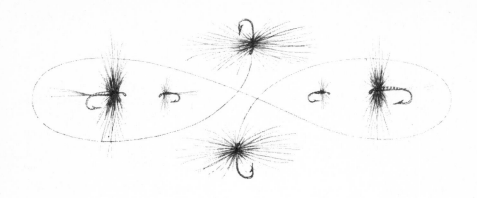

CHAPTER VII *Fishing with Spiders and Variants*

DURING THE season of 1946 I carried out an experiment that had been in my mind for a long time; to determine whether the dry-fly angler could limit himself to spiders and variants and still enjoy a reasonable success. Not that eliminating the use of the old favorites appeals to me particularly—I enjoy the variety that accompanies the changing of flies to solve various fly-fishing problems. But in order to determine exactly how effective the spiders and variants were, I had to use them exclusively. Except for a few changes to an imitation of the hatch for purposes of comparison, the spider and variant were the only flies used through the entire season.

The flies I used were from one to two and one half inches in diameter. They were tied on light No. 14 or 16 hooks, and only a few had a tail or a body. The spiders were either furnace or badger, or both mixed, and the variants a mixture of furnace and blue dun.

On a few occasions when the hatch was heavy and large fish were feeding steadily on the duns, an imitation of the natural was sometimes more successful than spiders or variants. But the largest fish I saw taken that season came to a big badger spider and the rod of Mead Schaeffer during a fine hatch. It was a lovely, bright female brown trout of about twenty inches, not weighed, as it was returned to the water.

I did not try to match the color of insects on the water when fishing the spiders during 1946, but fished them more as a lure than as an imitation. Nearly all the large fish that rose came to a moving fly rather than one floating conventionally. The variant was successful only when it was fished in the orthodox manner with no movement imparted.

Whether the results of my experiment have any real significance I can hardly say. At least they indicate what so many have suspected, namely that the number of fish taken in a season on spiders and variants will only vary little from that which would have been taken on the usual assortment of patterns, provided that in both cases the fishing was done with equal care and confidence. Now that the experiment is off my chest, I certainly would not care to repeat it. It is more fun to carry a variety of flies and spend at least part of the time tying Turle knots than to cast continually.

However, I was thoroughly convinced of one thing—that if I had to be limited to one dry fly it would be the spider, without any doubt. It can be used in so many more ways than the conventional fly; it is effective whether the water is high or low, colored or clear; and best of all, it brings up the large fish.

No doubt many anglers find spiders successful when cast and fished like any other dry fly. But in limiting themselves to that type of fishing they are apt to neglect the real function of this fly, that of being fished in movement. The average trout of decent size is cautious about rising. If he can be located and cast to repeatedly without any mistake, in the manner of George La Branche, he can sometimes be risen. But one should know *exactly* where the trout is to use this technique successfully. This necessitates a greater than ordinary knowledge of the water.

With the spiders, if one knows *approximately* where a good fish may be expected, one stands a good chance of raising the fish by working the fly. This is almost like fishing all the water with a wet fly. It is one of the very best ways of locating a large trout and, once risen, the angler stands an excellent chance of hooking him.

The spider is a great boon to the mediocre caster. It is almost impossible to bring it down heavily, due to its long hackles and consequent air resistance. This is why it is such a grand fly to use under bushes, where the line must be driven with force to shoot the flat loop essential in keeping the cast close to the water. Trout, particularly brown trout, often lie very near the bank, across the current from the angler. This necessitates skilful casting with the conventional type of dry fly to avoid drag. There is nothing quite so unattractive to either the fish or the angler as a dragging fly under these conditions. And if the trout be of decent size, such drag almost always puts him down.

With the spider, however, such a situation offers one of the best opportunities, as the drag is deliberately created rather than avoided. There is a great difference between the drag of a conventional fly, usually with the body in the water causing a heavy wake, and that of a spider cocked lightly up on the tips of its long stiff hackles, with the hook not touching the water at all.

When the spider is cast, it may alight flat with the hackles forming a circle and the hook down; the leader curved in the air between the eye of the hook and the water. This is an unattractive position for the leader as well as the fly. Some anglers are content to fish their spiders in this way but I have found that it raises very few trout. But if the angler tightens slightly on the line, the fly will quickly turn up onto the tips of its hackles. This motion is slight but deadly. To the trout it probably resembles a fly about to take off, and the rise will often come with a rush. Generally, the spider is a better lure when cast on its hackles. It is impossible to move it properly otherwise. And its greatest attraction is the lightness with which it moves.

I believe that the spider should be cast directly across stream, or down and across rather than up, or up and across. Then, when motion is given to it, it does not pull downstream in the manner of the usual drag but across. The long stiff hackles also allow it to be fished directly downstream, which can be very deadly.

As a matter of fact, it is surprising how really few fishermen ever fish the dry fly downstream. In salmon fishing it can be particularly deadly. The sight of a leader at times is almost sure to frighten them and hence they will come more readily to a fly floated down to them from above. It is not at all difficult to let the fly down to the fish by casting more line than necessary, and checking the rod midway, the resulting slack on the water allowing the fly to float down naturally. By waving the rod tip, line can be fed through the guides to lengthen the float.

When the conventional type of fly has passed well below the fish, the line should be pulled gently to one side, well away from the fish, before it is retrieved. It is best never to stand directly above the fish but to one side. When using the spider downstream, however, it is not necessary to pull it away from the fish before picking up; the fly can be retrieved in short jerks upstream or diagonally across and up. It can even be "hung" over the fish like a wet fly. Some one of these different styles of presentation is very apt to raise the trout.

One of the great attractions in fishing the large spiders, or skaters, is that frequently the trout clears the water in rising, taking the fly on the way down. This somehow proves that the spider excites the fish much more than the conventional fly, as one rarely sees a similar rise to an

orthodox type. This can be very disconcerting, as the angler is apt to strike too quickly on seeing a large fish in the air. But to me it is the rise of the fish that counts. It is by far the most interesting moment in the sport, and if I do not hook him, or if he breaks off, I still have experienced the supreme thrill.

Many anglers criticize the small hooks of spiders, and it is true that they make hooking more difficult, but once fastened they are not apt to pull out. I certainly had rather raise a big trout, even though I miss him, than fail to raise him at all. The spider seems to be the one fly which will bring large fish up several times if they miss at first, whereas I can remember very few brown trout of over a pound which rose more than once to the usual dry fly and the usual float.

The flies most effective on large fish are the very biggest spiders, those having a diameter of two inches or over. Unfortunately, it is difficult to obtain the hackles for them, as there are seldom more than a few on a neck which are long and stiff enough. This occasionally demands a sacrifice of color for stiffness. I sometimes tie spiders by using one hackle of the color I like, which may be a bit too soft, with another, stiffer one of some other color that will not spoil the effect.

To make spiders act properly on the water, one should use gut no heavier than 3x at the point and I like a long leader of about 12 feet with about three feet of fine gut next to the fly. Size 4x is even better than 3x, as any increase of the delicacy of the action or the high-riding qualities of the fly is an advantage. In using the conventional dry flies, I believe fine gut is important because of the added flexibility which gives the fly greater freedom in the stream currents, not because it is less visible. The fly is more apt to act naturally, following the tiny changes of current as a real insect might. This is why Lee Wulff uses thread for leaders, at times. He obtains a very natural float by throwing slack and allowing the currents to control the fly, the thread being so soft that it does not retard this natural movement.

It is surprising how often a rising fish which has refused the conventional fly will come to a spider. The change of *type* to one more like a lure than a natural fly is very apt to cause him to rise.

Variants are nearly as good a bet as spiders for general fishing when no hatch is on. Or they may be tied to resemble the color of the insect and fished to the rise. For many hatches they seem to be more lifelike to the fish than conventional patterns, particularly when imitating insects of delicate form and coloration. Their light pattern is reasonably close to that of many naturals and is more realistic than that of the orthodox fly. This is due to the long, sparse hackle, with the small, light hook being held free of the water. The very light, airy effect of the dressing as a whole is an improvement over most conventionally dressed flies.

In tying my variants I design them for the type of water to be fished. For still water little hackle is used; in fact the entire dressing is made as delicate as possible. For broken water I make them bushier, and of the very stiffest hackle. The variant should always ride high on the water, as it is much more effective than when half submerged or in the surface film.

My own experience has proved that better results are obtained when variants are used with little or no movement. Occasionally bouncing or bumping the fly, when first cast, can help to raise a stubborn fish. This is best done on broken water, of course. When fished over rising trout or on smooth water I allow the fly to float as naturally as possible.

I have had little success in trying to imitate the spinner of the natural fly. For one thing, it is usually right in the surface film, its wings flat, and thus the fish gets a much clearer view of it. My long-continued efforts to imitate one variety of spinner with all manner of dressings ended long ago with a score which I will not even mention. I have given up all attempts at copying this irritating little bug and instead have concentrated on the use of variants. I must say that even now the score remains lower than I would like, but at least it is a great improvement.

CHAPTER VIII *Flies and Impressionism*

TROUT STREAM insects have certain things in common. In the May flies we find some characteristics apparent in all of them. The most important of these characteristics is the type of color and texture.

If you will look closely at a live dun (not one in a specimen bottle) you will observe that his coloring is "impressionistic." It is built up of many tiny variations of tone such as we find in the paintings of Renoir, Monet and others of the impressionistic school of art. The body usually varies in color from back to belly and from thorax to tail. The thorax very likely contains little accents of color—bright pink, yellow and even bluish tones. The eyes in some naturals are brilliant dark blue or violet. Frequently the legs are spotted, and sometimes of strongly differing colors, the front pair being light and the others darker. All May flies have delicate veined wings and some, such as the March Brown and Green Drake, have very dark and distinct wing spots of brown or black. Add to all this the iridescence of the wing as it reflects the light, and it seems quite remarkable that the trout take our poor imitations at all.

As an artist, realizing how the intelligent use of color can give life to a picture, I feel that anglers are prone to neglect the possibility of using more living color in their flies. If an artist were to thoroughly mix certain colors to obtain a gray and then apply it to the canvas, the gray would be devoid of any lifelike quality. But, if he should apply the same colors directly to the canvas without mixing them beforehand, the result would have a great deal more vibration, light and life. At close range, the effect would be one of a mixture of colors. But at a slight distance they would appear close to the color and value of his original mixed gray, except that it would be alive and not dead.

The flies used for so discriminating a fish as the trout should, first of all, have the appearance of life. I am convinced that a lifelike effect can never be obtained by using materials which lack that quality. Impressionism in the materials as well as in the form of flies offers great advantages because it is based on the principles and discoveries of the impressionist painters. As they studied the form which reflected or absorbed light and thus took on certain color qualities of its surroundings, they were dealing in life, not death. Anglers should do the same.

We cannot take a brush and color our patterns as we would like them to be. But we can use more intelligence in our choice of materials. Good materials are what make a fly effective, other things being equal. Assuming reasonably skilful tying, our flies stand or fall on whether or not we employ proper materials in the proper way.

In many of our imitations the natural qualities of the insect are lost entirely. This is frequently due to the use of dyed materials, not mixed together but used separately. Occasionally the person who is clever with dyes can obtain a color which is excellent, and such materials sometimes work well. But too often the commercially tied patterns, done in mass production, make no attempt to do more than cover a hook with a mass of unrecognizable stuff, fit only for the wastebasket.

I should have begun this chapter by stating that almost any fly will take trout at times. We all know about the fishing contest winner who pulls out a monster on a home-made contraption of broomstraw, grocer's twine and fingernail parings. We should not be concerned with such exceptions because we know that for every trout caught by accident there are dozens taken by design.

The usual reason for poor flies doing well is that the angler has enough knowledge of the stream and cleverness in presentation to overcome the handicap. But I see no reason for setting an obstacle in the way of our sport unless, of course, we do not wish to catch fish. This point of view would be unique among anglers of my acquaintance.

The materials used for the wings of our dry flies are apt to be too heavy and opaque to properly suggest the natural. Although the subimago or dun has a reasonably opaque wing, it is still far removed from the heavy, thick feathers which adorn so many of the standard patterns. A great many American anglers are discontinuing the use of quill feather wings on their flies. They are either dispensing with them entirely or using wood duck or mandarin side feathers. There is no doubt that a more lifelike effect is achieved by such materials, as they break up the outline of the fly and lend the speckled look which is typical of many ephemera.

Wood duck and mandarin wings as tied by the modern angler are well divided, and are a great asset in cocking the fly properly. The vertical wing is apt to cause the fly to land on its side unless tied with great pains to secure absolute balance. For visibility too the divided wings of light speckled feathers are a help to the angler. He can see his fly better.

In many respects the wingless type of dry fly is as killing as the winged one, but it is hard to see. Recently, during an early hatch, I experimented with simple hackled patterns and found they killed well, even better in some cases than winged flies. But in poor light or broken water, they become very difficult to follow properly in their float, particularly if dun hackles are used, and I feel that the angler should always be able to see his fly in order to detect drag or any unnatural movement.

In recent years I have used the speckled side feathers of the Bali duck for winging some of my patterns. These feathers, while not as good in many respects as wood duck or mandarin, are darker in color and offer interesting possibilities. Certain ephemera have dark wings and in tying their imitations, a Bali wing is a closer color match to the natural besides having the same soft silhouette as wood duck. The markings of these feathers are amazingly delicate and lend a very insect-like look. They are also useful for some wet-fly patterns where a dark wing is desired.

Hackle points are probably the closest thing to the natural fly wing in appearance, and I have found them very effective for certain patterns. However, they are fragile and frequently one wing will break off, leaving the fly lopsided and useless. There is nothing quite so good for imitating the very light, pale duns. The glassy natural dun hackle point is amazingly lifelike.

I have found that in tying these feathers in, one should leave an eighth or a quarter of an inch of the barbules on the stem of the hackle. When it is tied in, these extra barbules will stand out at all angles, but they can be trimmed off. When tied down to the hook shank they reinforce the center shaft.

Another method of winging, very good for spinners or very delicate duns, is to use barbules stripped from the hackle and tied in, in a bunch, then separated and cocked as with wood duck.

We occasionally find flies tied with synthetic winging material, fabricated with veins, etc. In the showcase they sometimes appear quite lifelike, but I have never found them to be effective.

Hair is becoming more generally used for wings of flies, and there are certain types of hair which lend themselves very well to such use. Some time ago I was sent a sample of what was called Brazilian mouse-deer hair (the title alone would intrigue the inventive fly-tier!) which is an effective material for winging small wet and dry flies. It is of a lovely tan color and the tips of the hairs are speckled with white or cream. When on the fly its appearance is somewhat like that of mandarin or wood duck feathers.

In body materials I am a firm believer in the effectiveness and lifelike qualities of fur of some sort rather than silk or wool. These latter are not worth using for dry flies, for not only do they soak up water to a great extent, but their colors cannot be depended on, since they darken when wet. The hard outline or silhouette of a silk body is also a distinct disadvantage.

Wool has a softer outline against the light, but it is only good for wet flies due to its water-absorbing qualities. Some wool is fluorescent, that is, it glows when under ultraviolet light. Some anglers claim that wool is noticeably fluorescent at night or in the evening due to a certain amount of ultraviolet light being still present. But like the luminous bass lures the luminous fly has yet to show its advantage.

Fur may be easily blended, which is difficult if not impossible with many other materials. The mixed combination of colors to make the desired hue gives it a very lifelike quality. We have a great range of choice, due to the host of animals whose fur is useful for this purpose. Certain colors have to be dyed, but when blended with other dyed or natural colors, the effect is not one of a dyed material. The water animals, of course, are best for waterproof qualities. Seal's fur is my favorite as it has a wonderful sheen in the water as well as a very soft silhouette on the fly. It is not easy to spin on the tying silk as it is quite wiry in texture, but mixed with fox belly fur or some other soft dubbing, it works up beautifully.

The fly tier will find that he can save considerable time and trouble if he will make up fairly large supplies of the various mixtures of fur used in his patterns. If a new batch is made each time the tier needs a few more flies of a certain type, he will not only need to bring out a whole stock of furs but will have the trouble of matching the color each time.

This suggestion applies not only to the blending of fur but to the preparation of other materials used in quantity. A professional tier lays out all his materials before beginning actual construction of the fly. Feathers for the tail, dubbing and tinsel for the body, winging material and hackles are placed in convenient order. Hackles are stripped ready for tying in and if quill feather wings are to be used, the sections are cut out or stripped, ready for the winging operation.

In mixing fur for dubbing I generally make a little pile of each different color or material in the proper proportions. Then I take one pile of dubbing and shred it or pick it apart so that it falls onto another pile, turning the lower one over occasionally to distribute the mixture equally. Next I take up the pile of combined materials and pick it apart with the tips of the fingers, gradually mixing each material with the other. It may be necessary to repeat this picking process several times when using fur such as mole. Any very short-fibered material is rather difficult to combine properly with another. Turn the mass of dubbing over and over in the left hand and gradually pick over the entire supply, letting it drop into a new pile from the fingers of the right.

As the mixture takes on its combined color, one can easily determine whether it should have a bit more of one material or another, and this may be added as needed. It is best not to start the mixing operation with too much material, otherwise one may find himself in the situation of the house painter who, in attempting to match a color, ends with a gallon of paint when he needed only a quart. One may also find it necessary to spin a bit of the material and try it on a hook to see exactly how it looks, for frequently the dubbing looks quite different in the pile than on the fly body. The mixed dubbing, when completed, can be stored in labeled envelopes.

Similar preparations can be made with any fur which comes on a skin. Instead of stripping the fur each time a few flies are tied, it is best to prepare a good supply at one time. Hare's ear can be picked off and mixed, seal, muskrat, mole, fox and all the animal furs we usually buy attached to the hide. Quill can also be stripped and bleached or dyed for future use.

An excellent lifelike body can be made from the filaments of the cock pheasant's long tail feathers, and some killing patterns have been tied with this material. It has one disadvantage in its great fragility. Even with gold ribbing wound in the opposite direction, it seems to go to pieces very soon; therefore, I seldom use it for bodies. However, it is the best material I know of for the tails of nymphs, with the exception of the very tiny hackle found near the comb of the bird. Pheasant tail holds up reasonably well for this purpose and as I usually lose my nymphs before they are worn out, I continue to use it. When they are cast very close to shore, under branches and beside obstructions, the life of these little lures is a short one for me. But I am willing to risk their loss in order to make the casts which bring out the good trout.

We all know the effectiveness of peacock herl as a body material. It is truly impressionistic as it has the changeable shimmer and translucence of something alive, particularly under water. Hare's ear, another tried and true dubbing, is good alone or mixed with other materials such as seal, fox-belly or muskrat fur. The little spotted hairs combine with the softer pinkish hair at the base of the ear to make a wonderfully lifelike effect. It is used on my favorite dry-fly patterns as well as my nymphs and wet flies.

The mixed colors of dubbing, hare's ear with seal's fur, the combination of natural seal, dyed seal and muskrat are exceptionally effective. Bodies of these dubbings have the shimmer, the softly colored translucent quality of the insect. Dubbing such as seal's fur is excellent for wet flies. It gives the effect of something alive which carries little bubbles of air. It adds a tremendous amount of life to any fly.

Nearly all of my favorite fly patterns have gold ribbing. I use it for these good reasons: it is a great help in keeping the dubbing from being chewed or worn off; it gives a slightly segmented silhouette to the body of the fly; and by its tiny sparkles it suggests the shimmer of the insect. The ribbing I like best is the very finest bright gold *oval* tinsel. No doubt silver would serve the same purpose but I prefer gold, just for personal reasons. Flat tinsel is too weak; it breaks easily. And wire is so fine one is barely conscious of any color at all when it is mixed with the loose hairs of the dubbing.

Many of the flies that I see have too little body. Their bodies are not only too short but too thin. It seems to me that a fly body should suggest the juicy succulence of the natural, and furthermore I like a body with a certain *authority*. If the dubbing or other material is too tightly spun and wound the softness of silhouette is lost. No doubt the tight, hard bodies hold up well in use but it is more important that a fly body should suggest a good mouthful to the trout. The Wulff flies are excellent in this respect, having a decidedly rough, heavy look. They are great fish-getters. I do not believe in carrying body size to the point of clumsiness but feel that it should look like a good morsel to the fish.

The famous Tup's Indispensable is a fine example of an effective body.

The mixture of seal's fur (a substitute for the original dubbing) has a wonderful translucence in the water and many anglers will vouch for its killing qualities. I use it both as dry fly and nymph, and each has proved its worth many times over. This is a good example of an impressionistic fly.

When we come to the choice of hackle for our flies, particularly dry flies, we find considerably more difficulty in procuring good material. To obtain the proper color is one thing, but to find both color and quality —stiffness—is rare indeed. We all live in hope that by some strange turn of fortune we shall become the possessor of the ideal neck, the color neither too light nor too dark, the suggestion of red in the dun of the exact proportion, and the stiffness dangerous to our fingers. It is something we can dream of to the end of our lives as it will undoubtedly be still only a dream even then.

My own favorite colors for hackling the impressionistic type of flies are almost entirely of the cross-bred variety. The various mixtures of gray, tan, brown, black and white which occur in these seldom-found cocks are excellent for giving the fly a mixed-color look.

I had rather use a hackle of the right color and texture—the latter made up of the tiny speckles of color or tone which occur in a good natural dun, for instance—than one of better quality but of poor color even though some floating qualities and "light pattern" are sacrificed to a certain extent. By combining a fair quality hackle of proper color and one of poor color but greater stiffness, the fly can be made doubly effective.

We can also obtain good color combinations by using two hackles of different colors in order to get a mixed look. When, for example, one cannot obtain good cree hackle, which is a grizzly or Plymouth Rock hackle with considerable buff, ginger or red in it, a good approximation can be made by using one grizzly hackle and one ginger or red hackle wound on together. Badger combines well with ginger, red or dun and furnace or coch-y-bondhu mixes well with dun or grizzly. Once the angler sees how much more "buggy" his flies look with these mixed materials I am sure he will tie his new patterns and fish with considerably more confidence.

The fisherman who takes what sport he can find, who is not apt to devote much time to the collection of natural insects while on the stream and who prefers to let others do his research and experimentation is the man we most frequently meet with a flyrod. He may be allowed only a few week ends in the entire season, and he prefers to devote them to actual fishing rather than to the note-taking and close observation of the naturalist.

Many anglers feel that anything resembling work, other than wading a stream and hiking to and from their automobiles, is something to avoid if their fishing is to be pure pleasure. I fish only for fun myself and refuse to stop fishing to capture a natural unless I feel like it, or to take any notes whatever on the stream. So I can sympathize with these anglers who so seldom are allowed the opportunity of catching trout. Being a fortunate individual who spends on the average at least part of three or four days a week on the stream, I can hardly find reason for my laziness other than to say that if one does enjoy fishing for its own sake he should avoid any suggestion of making it a chore. As soon as the sport becomes a pursuit, or resembles anything other than sport itself, it loses its main attraction.

By this argument you might believe that I never bother to do anything other than cast a fly. This is certainly not true, as there are many times when nothing seems more pleasant than to spend a few hours studying a rising trout, looking for nymphs under stones or watching the emergence of the spinner from the dun on a bush along the stream. My idea of fun is to do these things when you wish, not when you should!

With such an angler in mind, I have tried to develop fly patterns that will cover most of his fishing. The hatches which he will encounter, at least on the Eastern streams, can be reasonably well matched and he should enjoy his sport without having to spend his time on anything but fishing.

Conditions on our streams are such that a great deal of the time there are no hatches of importance on the water. The angler chooses a good standard pattern, fishes all the water and takes a reasonable number of trout. He occasionally finds a rising fish which may be selective and which will need to be worked over. Or, if fortunate, he might be on the stream during a fine hatch of duns which he can imitate successfully and enjoy an angler's field day.

We have been given several very useful books on the important insects of our Eastern waters, and those of Preston Jennings, Art Flick and Charles Wetzel contain a great deal of information about naturals and their imitations. The dressings of their flies vary in some instances, possibly due to variations of the insect in the different localities. But usually trout feeding on the naturals will take the flies if they are fished in the localities for which they were designed.

The local variations in color and size of certain of the Ephemeroptera are quite surprising. Hatches also vary greatly in size from year to year. As surely as we are supplied with a pattern which killed well one season we shall find that the next year brings a disappointing scarcity of the natural and our full boxes are not of much use.

Many of our important trout-stream insects in the Eastern states are about of one size and can be imitated on a No. 12 or No. 14 hook. The naturals of the Light Cahill, Hendrickson and Gray Fox are all close in tonal "value" and of about the same size. By value I mean the degree of combination of light and dark, regardless of color, which makes up the general look of the fly.

In comparing the naturals of these patterns from a river in the Catskills and one in Pennsylvania or Vermont, one sometimes finds surprisingly strong differences. Often an entirely different pattern from the standard may be a closer imitation of such a local variation in the natural. As I am lazy about tying flies for one occasion, I should hate to think that I had to tie a new variation of the same fly for each stream I fish.

So long as we cannot be absolutely sure about how our flies look *to the fish,* we can only prove an imitation good by catching fish on it, not by comparing it with the natural in our own sight. In the supposed natural of the Quill Gordon, *Iron fraudator,* for example, the wings are of a decided lead color. The body is frequently reddish or brown. We all know that the imitation is a really great fly which will catch fish at almost any time. But when we compare the insect and the imitation we wonder how the latter was arrived at. The hackle color is a fairly close approximation of the color of the wings but the wood duck or mandarin feather wing does not approach the natural wing in color at all. The quill body is hardly true to life either, except that it suggests the strongly marked segments. Yet withal, we know that the fly is effective during the hatch.

Theodore Gordon said that he copied "the look of the fly on the water" and stressed this constantly in tying his imitations. I believe the Quill Gordon to be a good example of impressionism or approximation, the resemblance to the natural being achieved by combining certain colors in a way that appears lifelike to the trout.

Gordon said, "As a dry fly it [the Quill Gordon] is typical of certain ephemera." From this one must conclude that he intended the fly to imitate more than one insect. We also know that he continually varied the colors of the fly to suit different requirements.

In a letter to his friend Guy Jenkins dated March 14, 1913, Gordon wrote, "I like to use imitations of typical flies that fairly represent a *class* of insects. To have confidence in one's flies is half the battle. If a fly looks right to you on the water, it is apt to look right to the trout. It is the *effect* one wishes, not so much its appearance close to the human eye." (The italics are mine.)

These statements by an unusually observant angler have strengthened my belief in the killing qualities of flies which are not exact imitations of any one insect but an approximation of several. Although some of such flies may be reasonably close to a particular insect in form and color, they are designed primarily to simulate a group rather than a single variety.

There are certain of the well-known patterns based on the copies of the naturals which make fine general, all-season flies. These include the Hendricksons, Light Cahill, Quill Gordon and March Brown (American). Some of these patterns carry out the principles which I believe any good fly should maintain. They are "buggy" and impressionistic in appearance. Of course, this depends a great deal on how the fly is tied; one can hardly judge the effectiveness of a pattern by some bad example which not even remotely resembles the true dressing.

We are fortunate here in the East in having excellent fly tiers, people of experience and integrity in their work. They use good materials and their flies are surprisingly lifelike. In almost every case I know of, however, they work for individuals rather than the trade: the Darbees, Harry and Elsie; the two Dettes, Reub Cross, Elizabeth Greig and Alex Rogan, are but a few of a list of good craftsmen. These tiers conscientiously attempt to create artificials which carry out sound theory, and use materials which are a compliment to their efforts to obtain them, particularly in present times when some materials of quality are well-nigh unobtainable.

More recently there have appeared in the West some tiers who also carry out the tradition of fine workmanship and materials which has been typical of the better American tiers. Don Harger, of Salem, Oregon, Dan Bailey and Don Martinez are a few of the good ones.

Even the old standard patterns vary so much among tiers and districts that if the angler wishes a fly of an exact pattern he should always send a sample to the tier as a copy.

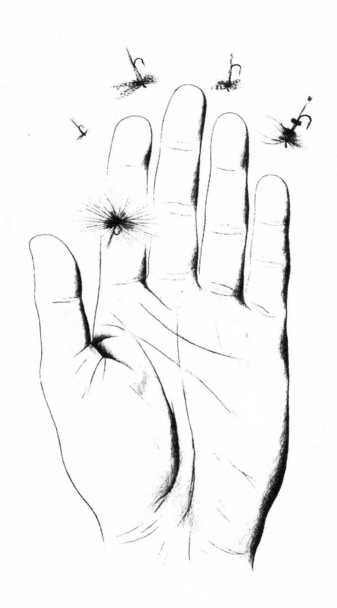

I have tried, in developing some patterns which I believe to be useful to the American fly fisher, to combine the qualities of the best materials with combinations of color and value which run in series from light to dark. With this small group of flies, and with the addition of several patterns of reputation, I believe the angler can cover all the conditions he will meet and keep his stock of flies to a minimum.

It is important that we consider any fly pattern for its results over long periods of time and not judge it by a few spectacular successes. Our flies should be useful during the hatches of naturals as well as for all-season fishing.

Frequently we find that during the early stages of a hatch, especially in the spring months when trout are hungry, we may take fish freely on a fly which seems to be different from the natural on the water. But if we follow the emergence of these flies, day after day, throughout the entire hatch, we will find that just any old fly will no longer take fish.

We frequently have an early hatch here in Vermont which continues for at least ten days. By the end of the third or fourth day a noticeable change has occurred. The trout which seemed so eager for our flies are not longer in such a taking mood. I have found it extremely difficult to raise fish at all on some of these occasions, and have been forced to do considerable experimenting with patterns before arriving at a fair solution.

During these trying periods, the more delicate the fly, the better it seems to work. This spring my best fishing was had with wingless flies, or flies with hackle-point wings or wings of hackle barbules. The hackle was kept fairly sparse and the fly reduced slightly in size. Where the natural was imitated actually by a No. 12 hook, I used a No. 13 and had better success.

My main criticism of the patterns of Mr. Jennings, which are excellent in many other respects, is the hook size, which I believe to be too large. We should try to offset the lack of realism in our imitations by reducing the size somewhat from the original. As our flies are so much more opaque and lack so many of the elements which characterize the insect, we can better achieve a resemblance, an impression if you please, by using a smaller hook and consequently less hackle to make a more delicate fly.

One day which is still fresh in my memory because it occurred only two weeks from this writing was one of those heartbreakers every angler encounters at some time or other. We had been having good luck during the hatch which had appeared about three o'clock each afternoon. On this particular day we returned to a place in the river where some good fish had risen a few days previously and where we had taken several really fine trout. At the proper time the flies appeared and the trout began feeding. We started fishing confidently over a pair of good fish, my wife somewhat below me in the river. The trout I had chosen for my particular efforts was on the edge of some slack near the far bank, and by his heavy swirls must have been a handsome fish.

After some time without rises we tried different variations of the fly. Still no action was forthcoming. I was particularly careful about drag, as I was familiar with the lie of my trout and knew from experience how they hated a dragging fly there. At last I heard from my wife the familiar sound which denoted a rise and a fish hooked, a combination of scream and triumphant yell.

You may be sure I redoubled my own efforts, as I could see t' at her fish was a good one. My next cast was a bit too far upstream, and a little puff of wind took it even farther than I intended and nearer the bank. The moment it touched, a trout had it, but not *my* trout! It was a pure fluke. I hadn't even known the fish was there, but at least I had hooked one. He turned out a decent fish all right, of about a pound or a little over and was picked up, unhooked and returned after a lively battle. My wife's trout was somewhat larger. So the laurels still rested on the wrong side of the family for my own comfort.

After things had quieted somewhat, *my* trout began rising again, sending out those heavy waves which denote a fish of real thickness of shoulder. After a great many casts, changes of fly to the variants, spiders and back to the original pattern again, I was growing greatly discouraged. It finally happened just when I was ready to call quits. I had cast above the fish, the fly had passed him a trifle, and in my disappointed carelessness I hurried the pickup. The fly began to drag and just as it speeded up on its slant downstream, the big fellow came at it mouth open. He didn't touch it, of course. I was much too good for him and succeeded admirably in pulling it away faster than he could travel. That was the end of that.

Unlike some anglers who tie their variants and spiders on large hooks, I adhere to the small hook sizes. In most patterns I use gold tinsel for body material or dispense with the body entirely, as in the large spiders or "skaters." It is important to fan out the hackle fore and aft on the fly to give a natural-appearing light pattern. With the small hooks of light wire, little hackle is necessary to float the fly properly. This helps to achieve correct light pattern and to aid in delicacy of presentation. The types employed on broken water, where they are sometimes fished in movement across and downstream, require more hackle.

The most effective variants I have used over many years have been combinations of furnace with dun, grizzly or cree, and badger with red or ginger. Occasionally a fly tied with dun or rusty dun is very good for calm or low water and difficult fish, although the dun and furnace mixture continues to be my best fish-getter under nearly all conditions.

The large spiders are similar in color, although I use dun hackle less than with the variants. They are nearly all mixtures of badger or grizzly with furnace, and with red and ginger added occasionally to help in stiffness when needed. These are tied with no body, and for rough water I use three hackles instead of two. I usually face the first two hackles so that the best side is next the curve of the hook. The last hackle is tied on as usual. This tends to keep the barbules from pulling down over the hook. To aid further in stiffening the hackles, I put a drop of lacquer at the base of the barbules in front and back.

Sometimes by altering the construction of a fly, trimming off part of the wings or hackle, it can be made more successful. There are times when it is best for the dry fly to lie directly in the surface film of the water. What Edward Hewitt calls 50-50 flies are of this type and are tied with the hackle greatly reduced on the bottom by trimming. It no doubt has the effect of the spent spinner when in the surface film, the hackles appearing as the outstretched wings of the natural.

One such pattern which proved to kill well on the Neversink was given to me by my friend Richard Hunt, an angler of real prowess, one of the best of my acquaintance. The fly was based on the Tup's, as the body was identical, the difference being that a dark grizzly hackle and a tail of the same color were used. It was tied on a small hook, a No. 16, and the hackle cut away on the bottom in a wide V so that the hackles bent sufficiently to allow the body to rest on the water.

Mr. Hunt, by the way, seems to do much less false casting in dry-fly fishing than ordinarily seen. In fact a great deal of the time he uses no more than the usual pick-up and delivery of the wet-fly cast; this results in a lower-floating fly than ordinarily fished, and particularly in using flies of the 50-50 type he used this method when we fished together.

Every dry-fly fisher who is familiar with the hatches of the large May flies, the Green Drakes, which are so heavy on the Beaverkill early in June, probably has his favorite imitation. No doubt this big natural, the largest of our May flies, has been copied or simulated with more variety than any other fly. Some of the imitations are incredibly large and bushy, and every degree of color theory that can be summoned by the creative fly tier is tried out. It is probably more difficult to imitate successfully a natural as large as this ephemera as the trout can so easily detect fraud in a large fly. But of course there are always days when the fish are so intent on gorging themselves that they lose their natural caution and are not put down by a clumsy imitation. So at least part of the time, almost any of these inventions will take fish.

We hear at times of hatches of these large flies which become news, piling up in the streets of towns, impeding traffic and becoming altogether a great nuisance. Not until last summer did I ever witness anything so spectacular. We were driving across the continent and had stopped for the night at an auto camp on Lake Erie. During the later afternoon and evening, these large ephemera—whether *guttulata* or some other I could not determine—hatched in such incredible numbers as literally to drive us indoors. The street cleaning department actually had to shovel them up and carry them away; traffic was slowed and the entire affair resembled more a heavy snowstorm than a hatch of insects. We watched hundreds break their subimago skins and emerge as the final lovely and delicate spinners with transparent wings and waxy white bodies. My greatest regret was that there were no trout streams nearby. It seemed a shame that such grand fish food, the flies that we look forward so greatly to seeing in our streams, should have to be disposed of by the shovels of the street cleaning department.

Among imitations of this fly, several have surprised me by their lack of realism. One good angler of my acquaintance made no attempt at a direct copy but used a very large Pink Lady bivisible, about No. 8. He seemed to take as many trout as most. Art Flick, an excellent angler and a beautiful fly tier, employs a large variant.

When I last fished during this hatch, some years ago, I tried several patterns which were closer to the form as well as the color of the natural. I usually tied them on a long-shanked No. 10 May fly hook with a body of cream dubbing gold-ribbed, wood duck wings and a grizzly hackle dyed a pale greenish yellow. The wings were sometimes made fanwing style.

I am quite sure that out of the literally dozens of different patterns I have seen which were tied to imitate this fly, there were no two alike. And most of them took fish, a few more than others, presentation or stream knowledge accounting for the better scores. Unfortunately I have missed this hatch for a number of years, as the streams I fish mostly at present do not see the big Drakes in any numbers. I surely would welcome an opportunity to see once more the big wild brown trout filling their bellies with these succulent morsels. It does not always pay off too well, but it never fails to increase the pulse.

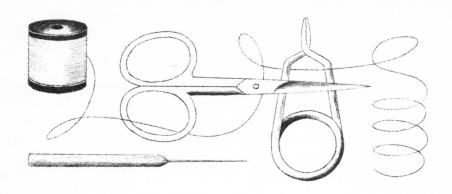

CHAPTER IX *Dry Flies*

I AM INCLUDING in this chapter a list of my favorite dry flies and their dressings. These are the flies most generally useful throughout the season both for imitating the hatches of natural insects and for fishing the water when few flies are present. Along with the flies of my own design, I am including a list of what I consider the most useful standard patterns, either because they carry out my theory of "impressionism" or because over many years of use they have proved their practical worth.

The principal idea in developing my own group is to have the flies in a color gradation, from light to dark, which will include most variations we find in the important naturals. By listing them in this order, it will be found easier for the angler to keep the sequence in its color relationship.

In nearly every one of these patterns, as well as in some of the "standards," I vary the dressings slightly from time to time when I find that the natural is thereby more closely approximated. But usually the dressings given will be found adequate for most hatches familiar to Eastern waters. I make a constant search for new and more effective materials which might give a better and more lifelike effect than the present dressings, and from season to season there are usually changes for the better in these designs.

Most of the patterns of my own design are most useful in sizes 14, 13 and 12. The majority of insects which they approximate occur in those sizes. I have, however, listed a range of useful hook sizes; occasionally these extremes are effective. Frequently a change of size is more important than a change of pattern.

In the West, particularly at high altitudes, the smaller sizes are often more useful. When temperatures of both air and water are apt to be low the insects seem to be smaller. The seasons for emergence are short and the water is usually clear. This all results in a preponderance of tiny insects best imitated by 14's, 16's and even 18's and 20's. Very large trout feed freely on these small naturals and often rise more confidently to small imitations than to the usual Western dry fly of large bushy construction.

The West also produces those amazing hatches of large caddis and stone flies which bring out numbers of the bigger trout. I have not included dressings of these flies here, but they are usually tied on hooks of about No. 8 or 6, with hair wings. Fox squirrel is good, and I have used some bodies made of kapok, an excellent floater, which can either be dyed to the color desired or used as a base under the dubbing or other material. The wings in any stone or caddis pattern should be tied flat or tent shaped over the back. In the caddis imitations the hackle is best tied palmer style, over the entire body.

In the following group, the flies are listed from light to dark, and I have inserted the standard patterns where I believe they best fit into this category of color gradation. My own list follows:

Number one:

TAIL	Pale dun hackle barbules.
BODY	Very pale cream fox-belly fur, ribbed with narrow oval gold tinsel.
WINGS	Hackle points from a light, glassy natural dun.
HACKLE	Very light cree, or one pale ginger and one light grizzly hackle wound so as to mix the colors.
HOOK SIZES	16, 14, 12.

Number two:

TAIL	Light brassy or rusty dun hackle barbules or a mixture of light ginger and light dun.
BODY	Light buff or pale tan fox-belly fur mixed with natural seal's fur and a small amount of hare's ear, ribbed with narrow oval gold tinsel.
WINGS	Wood duck, light.
HACKLE	One light cree and one medium dun hackle.
HOOK SIZES	16, 14, 12.

Number three:

TAIL	Medium cree hackle barbules or a mixture of ginger and grizzly.
BODY	Natural seal's fur mixed with bright yellow seal's fur, fox belly fur dyed yellow or dyed mohair. The color should be a light yellow but not too strong and should have a mixed look.
WINGS	Wood duck. I originally tied this wing with medium dun hackle points but recently changed to wood duck. Both materials are good, however, and the dressing can be adapted to local requirements.
HACKLE	Light rusty dun, or one ginger and one medium dun hackle.
HOOK SIZES	16, 14, 12.

Number four:

TAIL	Cree hackle barbules, or a mixture of ginger and grizzly.
BODY	Natural seal's fur mixed with dyed red seal, a little hare's ear and a little muskrat fur. The color should be a grayed, mixed pink. Ribbed with narrow oval gold tinsel.
WINGS	Wood duck preferably, or light-colored mandarin speckled side feathers.
HACKLE	A mixture of one cree hackle and one medium natural dun.

This fly will approximate certain pinkish-bodied naturals, and is even useful for some of the spinners with pink or reddish 'bodies.

HOOK SIZES   16, 14, 12.

Number five:

TAIL	Dark cree, or a mixture of red brown and grizzly.
BODY	Hare's ear, using the short speckled hairs on the ear and the pinkish tan hair at the base of the ears. It should have a decided mixed "buggy" look. Ribbed with narrow oval gold tinsel.
WINGS	Mandarin or wood duck.
HACKLE	Dark cree or a mixture of red-brown and grizzly.
HOOK SIZES	18, 16, 14, 12, 10.

This fly is the most generally useful of the group.

Number six:

TAIL	Dark rusty dun hackle barbules.
BODY	A mixture of dark muskrat or mole and some red-brown fur such as dyed seal's fur, to get a body of a brownish gray color, rather dark. Ribbed with narrow oval gold tinsel.
WINGS	This wing can be varied somewhat but my preference is for Bali duck side feathers. I also use bronze mallard and dark mandarin.
HACKLE	A natural rusty dun, or one fairly dark natural dun and one red brown hackle mixed together.
HOOK SIZES	18, 16, 14, 12.

Number seven:

This fly is designed for use when trout are feeding on midges or very small flies, as so often occurs on the "flats" during the evening. It can either be tied as a variant, with a slightly larger hackle than the size of hook calls for, and with a tail, or with no tail. It can also be made with or without a body. There hardly seems to be any choice as all variations work well.

TAIL	Very dark dun or black hackle barbules.
BODY	Very dark. I frequently use black tying silk, making a very small short body.
WINGS	None.
HACKLE	Very dark dun or black, either conventional proportions to the hook size or larger as preferred. I like dun best.
HOOK SIZES	18, 20, 22.

This selection of patterns, while covering a wide range of color and value in approximating trout stream insects, would hardly be complete without the addition of some of the best standard patterns. Those which have proved their worth for many years, both as flies for fishing all the water and for use with hatches, I am including here with the dressings as I tie them, arranged in order from light to dark:

Number one: Light Cahill.

TAIL	Ginger hackle barbules, fairly light.
BODY	Light creamish-buff belly fur from the red fox.
WINGS	Wood duck or light mandarin.

HACKLE	Ginger hackle—fairly light.
HOOK SIZES	16, 14, 12, 10.

Number two: Light Hendrickson or Henrickson.

TAIL	Medium dun hackle barbules.
BODY	Light pinkish tan fur from belly of red fox.
WINGS	Wood duck or mandarin.
HACKLE	Medium natural dun.
HOOK SIZES	16, 14, 12, 10.

Number three: Quill Gordon.

TAIL	Medium dun hackle barbules.
BODY	Stripped quill from the eye of the peacock feather, light, and with decided dark stripe. If quill is too dark it can be bleached in peroxide of hydrogen.
WINGS	Wood duck or mandarin.
HACKLE	Medium natural dun.
HOOK SIZES	18, 16, 14, 12, 10.

The Quill Gordon can be varied somewhat in dressing by using hackle of light, medium and dark shades on various patterns. As the naturals are apt to vary considerably, this will be found useful to approximate the fly on the water.

Number four: March Brown (American).

TAIL	Light red or deep ginger hackle barbules.
BODY	Can be made in several ways. Two of the best are: (1) Pinkish tan fur from belly of red fox mixed with a little hare's ear and a touch of dyed yellow seal's fur or yellow mohair. Ribbed with narrow oval gold tinsel or brown silk thread. (2) Hare's ear ribbed with light yellow floss silk. The ribbing should be narrow.
WINGS	Mandarin, rather dark and strongly marked with black bars.
HACKLE	Light red mixed with medium or dark grizzly.
HOOK SIZES	14, 12, 10.

Number five: Adams.

TAIL	Red brown and grizzly hackle barbules.
BODY	Muskrat.

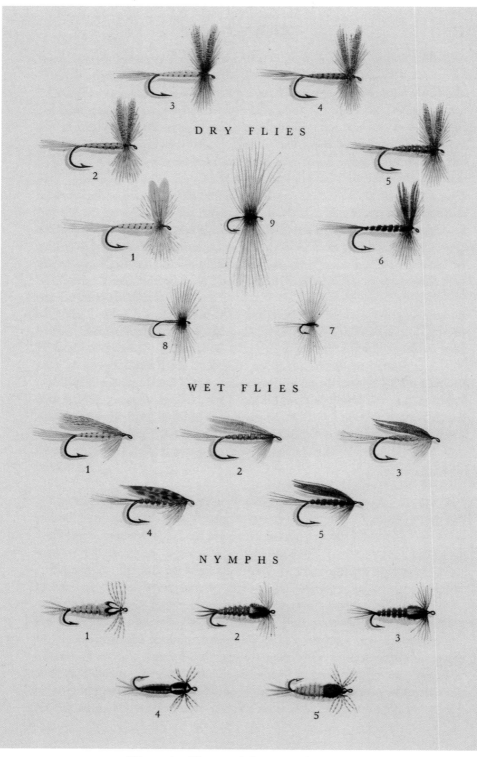

DRY FLIES

WET FLIES

NYMPHS

Plate A: Classic Atherton Fly Ties

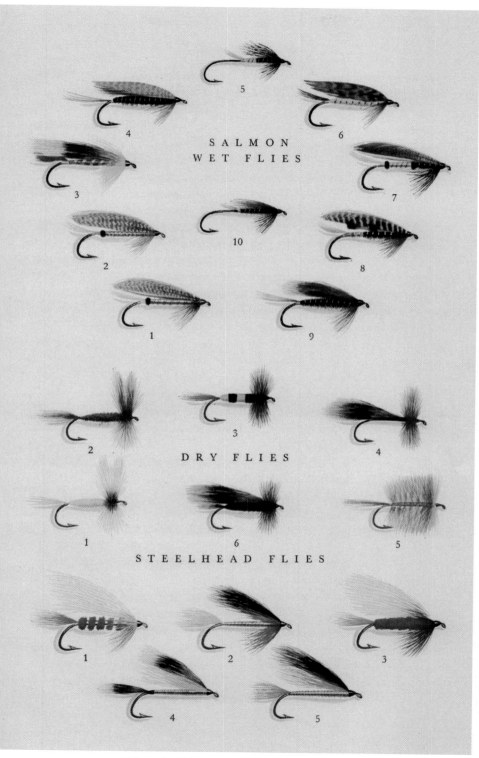

SALMON
WET FLIES

DRY FLIES

STEELHEAD FLIES

Plate B: Classic Atherton Fly Ties

WINGS	Hackle points from a medium grizzly cock tied spent wing fashion.
HACKLE	A mixture of medium grizzly and red brown hackles.
HOOK SIZES	16, 14, 12, 10.

Number six: Gray Wulff.

TAIL	Brown bucktail or Chinese deer tail.
BODY	Muskrat tied rather heavy and rough.
WINGS	Brown bucktail or Chinese deer tail.
HACKLE	Medium natural dun.

In the small sizes and occasionally in the larger ones, I prefer fox squirrel tail for both tail and wings of this fly. It has a more decided orange color and seems to be very effective.

HOOK SIZES 14, 12, 10, 8.

Following are the dressings for my favorite variants:

Variant number one: Cream Variant or Honey Variant.

TAIL	Cream or light buff colored hackle barbules.
BODY	Flat gold tinsel.
HACKLE	Cream or light buff. The best color of all is a natural honey dun.
HOOK SIZES	16, 14.

Variant number two: Tups Variant.

TAIL	The hackle used for both tail and hackle of this fly as I tie it is a pale dun of a brassy shade with faint markings of grizzly. It is a very unusual color and seldom encountered. A good substitute would be either a very pale cree hackle or a mixture of tan or buff and very light grizzly.
BODY	A short segment near the tail of bright yellow silk floss, then the body of a mixture of natural seal's fur and dyed red seal's fur to get a pinkish tan color.
HACKLE	Same as tail.
HOOK SIZES	16, 14.

Variant number three:

| TAIL | Medium natural dun hackle barbules. |
| BODY | Flat gold tinsel. |

HACKLE   One medium natural dun and one furnace hackle
             mixed together.
HOOK SIZES   16, 14.

Variant number four:
TAIL   Medium dun or rusty dun hackle barbules.
BODY   Flat gold tinsel.
HACKLE   Medium natural dun or rusty dun.
I sometimes tie this fly with a quill body like the Quill Gordon, but
prefer the gold.

Variant number five:
TAIL   Cree hackle barbules.
BODY   Flat gold tinsel.
HACKLE   Cree hackle—can be either light, medium or dark; they
             all work well. Or it can be a mixture of red and grizzly
             hackle.
HOOK SIZES   16, 14.

My dressings for the spiders which I prefer are given below:

Spider number one: Badger hackle.
Spider number two: A mixture of badger and furnace or badger and
                         red.
Spider number three: Cree hackle or a mixture of red and grizzly in
                         varying shades.
Spider number four: Furnace.
Spider number five: Furnace   yellow body.
                         Body   yellow; the same as dry fly number
                                   three, small and short.
                         Hackle   furnace.

The last spider was designed after a suggestion by Edward Hewitt.
There were so many flies on the Neversink which had yellowish-colored
bodies that we frequently used this color in our imitations. It seemed to be
effective then, and since has proved very good on other waters. There is
just enough suggestion of color on the body to add to its attractiveness.

All of these spiders are tied with hackle varying from about one inch to about two and one-half inches in diameter. The yellow-bodied pattern I use only in the smaller diameters.

The tying silk used for all of these dry flies should be chosen to harmonize as nearly as possible with the color of the fly, particularly the body. For example, I prefer orange on the March Brown, yellow or cream on the Light Cahill, etc. Lightly spun dubbing is translucent and frequently the silk will show through. Impressionistic color effects can be achieved by combining analogous or complementary colors together, depending on the desired effect. An interesting combination using complementary colors together is to spin light blue gray dubbing on primrose yellow tying silk. Particularly when wet, this results in a lovely, elusive olive tint, reminiscent of natural insect coloration.

Avoid black or dark silk where a light colored dubbing is used. White silk is generally very useful and has practically no effect on the light and medium colored furs. Also white comes in very fine sizes and is easier to obtain than many other colors.

Hold your dry fly against the light and examine the effect of the spun dubbing. Never forget that the trout almost invariably sees it thus. And try the wet fly in water, observed from above as well as against the light. You may well be surprised at the comparison between a well constructed and colored fly, with properly spun dubbing, to one knocked together just anyhow.

In places where the caddis and stone flies are present in sufficient numbers to affect the fishing, I suggest that anglers experiment with palmer-hackled flies of various colors and mixtures of colors. I have not used any caddis or stone fly imitations for some time due to the lack of these insects in daylight hours on the streams which I frequent.

One could easily make a series of caddis patterns adequate to handle such hatches, using three variations in color from light to dark, either with or without wings. I personally prefer a plain, hackled fly or one with a hair wing such as the Western bucktail caddis.

A mixture of ginger and grizzly or light cree hackle over a yellowish body would do for one. A darker shade of ginger or red over an orange colored body for a second and a dark cree or mixture of red and grizzly or plain red over brown for a third. All of these could be winged with either bucktail (or deer-body hair, which is better), fox squirrel tail, red squirrel tail, the hair of the mouse deer mentioned before or some other hair with insect-like qualities.

For the wet caddis, hair is a very good material if wings are used. It might be more desirable to use wings since the fly underwater is viewed with more clarity. There are several varieties of hair, such as monkey, which have a decided speckled or mottled look, and have mobility in the water. If feathers are used, the same type of mottled effect should be tried for. Hen pheasant wing feathers, speckled hen, grouse and similar feathers are good. The wing, of course, should be tied nearly flat on the back, not sloping or upright.

The stone flies could be designed in similar fashion, although some prefer not to tie their hackles palmer style for these flies.

These are only suggestions which should be carried through experimental stages by the angler and developed to suit his needs. Ordinarily I should choose a variant or spider if no duns were on the water. The few caddis present have not affected my fishing to the extent that these long-hackled flies would not take trout under such conditions.

In recent years, the flies having deer hair or caribou hair bodies have done excellent work, and sometimes it pays to include a few patterns of this type. The imaginatively christened "Rat-faced McDougal" is one, and although I rarely employ this type of fly, my friends vouch for its effectiveness. It is slow to tie, with the rather complicated body construction, but

Legend for color plate on inside front cover

DRY FLIES

NUMBERS 1 to 6 show the author's series of dry flies, standard tie
NUMBER 7   small dun or black variant
NUMBER 8   variant number 3 in text
NUMBER 9   spider number 2 in text

WET FLIES

Showing numbers 1 to 5 in text

NYMPHS

NUMBERS 1, 2 and 3 show author's nymph patterns (three quarter top view)
NUMBER 4   Collins hard-bodied nymph number 1
NUMBER 5   Collins soft-bodied nymph number 2 (both shown three quarter top view)
All fly patterns are slightly larger than actual size

the amateur fly-tier is rarely pressed for time in his work and usually likes to experiment.

Another unusual type of dry fly made with hair rather than hackle is the hair spider. I have not fished it sufficiently to determine whether it is any improvement over the conventional spiders, but it seems to be equally successful, and is an excellent floater. When good large hackles are hard to find, one might experiment a bit with hair to see what can be done this way. I have used only deer body hair, or bucktail hair; the latter, when stiff enough, seems to be better. It is tied on the hook as in making a body like the McDougal, but not clipped off short. It is important to choose hair of the proper length and to place it on the hook so that when the thread is pulled tight and the hairs stand out in a circle from the hook shank, they are of the right length. One can easily make the hair slope forward by wrapping thread behind it. When fished, it will tend less to pull down over the curve of the hook.

If the reader is unfamiliar with the methods used in tying these hair bodies, instructions are available in the *Fly Tying Manual* put out by Herter's of Waseca, Minnesota. Most fly-tiers are already familiar with such techniques and I am therefore not including them here.

All of the suggestions I have made will be best tried out in the reader's own fishing grounds and altered according to the particular requirements found there. Bearing in mind the natural qualities of materials, the impressionistic look rather than the slavish copy, there is no reason why any intelligent angler and fly-tier should not succeed in developing his own best patterns.

Undoubtedly some anglers will wonder when my group of dry flies should be used, and how. These flies were designed to cover nearly all conditions but there are a few suggestions which may help in their use.

During the Spring, in May and early June, trout are apt to be rising to hatches. When these hatches are on the water, it is a simple matter to use the fly that approaches the natural most closely. It is important, however, for the angler to be sure he has examined the right insect, that which the trout are actually taking. Often two or three varieties are on the water at the same time. Until they are examined closely, one may waste considerable time in determining to what the trout are rising. Too, the hatches may vary in different parts of the stream. The angler who changes his location and continues to use the same fly, when the fish are taking a different natural, is due for disappointment. Male and female insects of the same variety may vary considerably, and it might be that the trout prefer one to the other. Close observation before making decisions is the best advice. The least the angler can do is to be sure what is happening on the stream before he ties on his imitation.

Later in the season, when hatches become fewer and of less variety, one may choose his patterns according to experience on that stream, the level of the water, its clarity and other factors. It would hardly be advisable to put on a No. 18 or 20 during a freshet, or use a large, bushy fly on a shallow flat. But even then, trout being such unpredictable creatures, it is hardly safe to make a rule. The angler can only determine what is effective by trying it.

Some of my patterns I use a great deal, others infrequently. But then, of course, the streams I fish may not be similar to those fished by another. I can only advise that, within reason, the following suggestions will be found to apply to the "average" trout waters.

No. 1 is good for some of the hatches of very pale coloration and transparency. It is useful as a general fly on still water, and is good in the evening.

No. 2 is similar in many ways but is a better imitation of the duns of some varieties which have darker or more opaque wings. I use this fly more than No. 1 as a general fly. I also use it without wings on certain occasions when fish are very difficult.

No. 3 is primarily a fly to approximate those insects which have distinctly yellow bodies. There are many of these occurring on some streams, one of which is the Neversink.

No. 4 is a very useful general pattern. It contains elements common to many insects and, next to No. 5, is the fly I use the most. The "value" or degree of light and dark of this fly and of No. 5 make them successful, due to the fact that they approximate the "buggy" qualities inherent in many insects. This pattern imitates certain spinners well.

No. 5 is the best fly in the group. It has stood up over many years as the best "general" fly I have used. It is good in all kinds of water, and in all sizes. It killed extremely well on landlocked salmon in Maine and on all varieties of trout in the West as well as in the East. If I could have only one fly of conventional design (not a spider or variant) it would be this fly. It is really astonishing how many hatches can be imitated by this fly, even though to the eye it seems to be too dark for some. But the trout take it well, so I will not question why and only conjecture that it may be because of its slightly greater "solidity," a sort of "accent" among the real duns.

No. 6 is a good early season fly, as many of the first hatches which appear are small and dark. It is also best in the small sizes. Excellent on still water in sizes 18 or 20, but naturally difficult to tie that small. Size 18 is about as small as I use this fly as a rule, going to the little, dark, hackle pattern instead when using 20's or 22's.

No. 7 is self-explanatory. Its main function is for raising that stubborn fish which has refused everything else!

The standard patterns are so well known that I will make no comment on their use. Every angler undoubtedly has his own preferences without my advice. The variants and spiders have been touched upon in the chapters devoted to that type of fly, and my choice has already been mentioned.

All the flies listed in this and other chapters can be obtained from the following fly-tiers. I have personally tied the patterns given them as standards.

E. B. and H. A. Darbee, Livingston Manor, N. Y.

Angler's Roost, Chrysler Bldg., New York, N. Y.

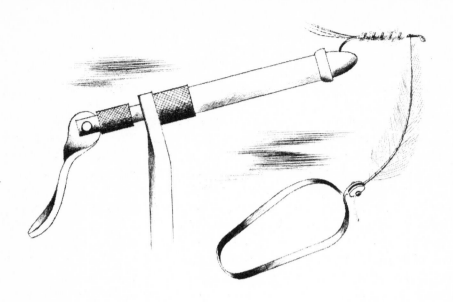

CHAPTER X *Wet Flies*

ANGLERS HAVE been using the wet fly since fly fishing was first practiced. The earliest forms of flies were similar to those popular today. They had a body, wing and hackle, or in some cases a hackle alone without the wing. The conventional wet fly still enjoys the widest use of any type in almost every locality.

Actually trout feed more on the nymph than on the winged fly beneath the surface. The nymph is apt to be more plentiful, and the artificial, when properly fished, is usually the more killing lure. But the angler who goes fishing only a few times each season will usually employ the standard wet-fly cast, with dropper, and will fish in the orthodox manner. He will probably catch fish that way although he may have a suspicion that his technique could be improved upon.

We know that the conventional wet flies are effective, but about all we can say as to the reason is that the fly represents something alive to the fish. If it has insect-like coloration and appearance in the water, if it moves in a lifelike manner and if it is presented to the fish so that he will be interested rather than alarmed, the results are apt to be reasonably successful.

The fish can view the wet fly, or any object below the surface, with a better chance of detecting fraud, due to the fact that his vision is much less affected by the distortion and refraction of light. Hence wet flies should be as lifelike as possible. The ordinary commercial wet flies are seldom tied with this consideration in mind. Often they are made of excessively opaque material or their color is lacking in insect-like qualities. Materials for flies fished below the surface should be translucent when wet. The body materials especially should be of the sort that will capture air bubbles and thus simulate the natural submerged fly.

The solid colored quill feather wings are seldom as "buggy" as the side feathers of the mallard, wood duck and mandarin, or the mottled feathers of pheasant, grouse, speckled hen, etc. And as in the dry fly, single colors in hackle such as brown or red-brown are rarely seen in the natural. The legs of the fly are almost invariably made up of several tones of color and sometimes of greatly contrasting ones.

The series of wet flies given here is based on principles similar to those affecting dry flies. These flies are designed to cover a range of colors and values which will include many of the insects found on our streams and will be useful throughout the season. The flies are listed from light to dark.

Number one:

TAIL   Light cree hackle barbules.

BODY   A mixture of natural seal's fur and dyed yellow seal's fur or mohair. (This body is the same as that in the dry fly numbered three of my series.) Ribbed with narrow oval gold tinsel.

WINGS   Brazilian mouse deer hair, or the short speckled hairs at the base of the fox squirrel tail.

HACKLE   Light cree.

HOOK SIZES   14, 12, 10.

Number two:

TAIL   A few fibres from the wood duck side feather.

BODY   A mixture of natural seal's fur, muskrat, dyed red seal's fur and a little hare's ear. Ribbed with narrow gold tinsel. This body is the same as that on the dry fly numbered four of my series.

WINGS   Wood duck or light mandarin.

HACKLE   Dark ginger or light red, tied quite sparse.

HOOK SIZES   14, 12, 10, 8.

Number three:

TAIL	Wood duck or mandarin fibres.
BODY	Hare's ear mixed with a little natural seal's fur to lighten it a bit. Ribbed with narrow oval gold tinsel.
WINGS	Bali duck side feathers. A good substitute is either finely barred teal or widgeon. It should be fairly dark.
HACKLE	Light cree or a mixture of ginger and grizzly.
HOOK SIZES	14, 12, 10, 8.

Number four:

TAIL	Dark cree hackle, or a mixture of red-brown and dark grizzly.
BODY	Hare's ear, tied rough and ribbed with narrow oval gold tinsel.
WINGS	Feather from the hen pheasant (ringneck) secondary. It should have a decided mottled look.
HACKLE	Dark cree or a mixture of red-brown and dark grizzly.
HOOK SIZES	14, 12, 10, 8.

Number five:

TAIL	Bronze mallard.
BODY	A mixture of muskrat or mole and some reddish brown fur such as seal or polar bear dyed to shade. (This body is the same color as the dry fly numbered six in my series.) Ribbed with narrow oval gold tinsel.
WINGS	Bali duck. Dark teal or bronze mallard could be substituted.
HACKLE	Rusty natural dun.
HOOK SIZES	16, 14, 12, 10.

To this group I usually add the following standard patterns which have proved successful:

Number one: Light Cahill.

The dressing is the same as the dry fly but tied wet, with much less hackle, generally thinner construction and a sloping wing.

Number two: Hewitt stone fly.

TAIL	Fibres of wood duck or mandarin, rather short.

BODY	Hare's ear mixed with pinkish-tan colored fox belly fur, ribbed with yellow floss silk. The rib should be quite distinct.
WINGS	Hen pheasant secondary wing feather tied tent-shape over the back.
HACKLE	Red-brown, just a few turns and the hackle clipped off at top and bottom leaving only that at the side.
HOOK SIZES	14, 12, 10.

Number three: Quill Gordon.

The dressing is the same as the dry pattern, but kept sparse and with a sloping wing.

Number four:	Leadwing Coachman.
TAIL	None.
BODY	Bronze peacock herl.
WINGS	A dark quill feather from the black duck, coot or some other dark dun feather tied tent-shape over the back.
HACKLE	Dark furnace or cochy-bondhu.
HOOK SIZES	12, 10.

I rarely use any other wet flies than these given above, and in fact, I had rather use a nymph when fishing beneath the surface. Nymphs are based on a more lifelike form and are certainly more prevalent in the trout's diet than either the drowned fly or the live one which has emerged from the nymphal shuck and is swimming to the surface.

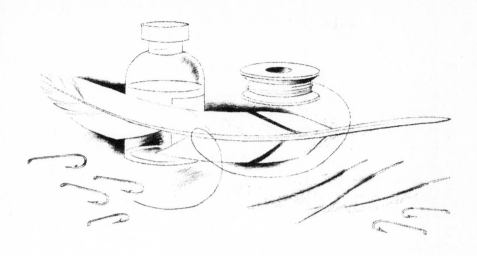

CHAPTER XI *Nymphs*

TO FIND out what the nymphal form of the fly is like, all one needs to do is to turn over a few stones along the edge of the stream. In water where hatches occur in sufficient quantity to produce a decent food supply, nymphs abound under stones and in the gravel or silt of the bottom. An hour or two spent at this interesting research will usually prove why the trout's diet is made up largely of underwater life. In some waters the amount of insect larvae and pupae seen on the bottom is amazing, and any number of varieties may be found.

The chief difficulty is to know what is most important in the trout's food supply. Of course by opening the stomachs of the fish we can identify the types of nymph, but there is still room for doubt as to how to imitate them.

I have had best success with artificials similar to the dry flies and wet flies, that is, a general type rather than a specific one. Most of my nymph fishing is done when only a few flies are on the water. At such times trout are not apt to be so selective. When a hatch appears, the short period before the emergence of the duns can be fished best with a close imitation of the natural nymph, although even at that time the impressionistic nymph of the general type is often successful.

Following my own experience, choice for that early pre-dun stage would be the dry fly. I have frequently tried a reasonably good imitation of a nymph, then followed it with one of the dun, and have come to regard the dry fly as the more useful, particularly as I had rather fish it, any time, than the nymph.

Recently a good friend and excellent angler, Wendle Collins—"Tom" to his friends—was kind enough to send me a series of nymphs which are probably the best I have ever seen. They have the "buggy" look and are amazingly realistic without being slavish in copying the natural. Mr. Collins was also generous enough to allow me to include this group of artificials and their dressings in my book. I can vouch for his powers of removing many and large trout from various streams and I am sure that his artificials are at least partly responsible.

My only objections, which are relatively slight, to these lovely creations are that they are quite difficult to tie, and that in some cases I would prefer a more impressionistic, mixed material.

When fishing with a nymph, I find it exceedingly difficult to keep my boxes well stocked, as my losses sometimes exceed production. As so many of my best brown trout are taken by casting the nymph very close to the bank and under overhanging branches, I discover frequently that the risks necessary to the proper presentation result in many flies hung up and never recovered.

To offset this rather unfortunate aspect of my nymph fishing, I have adopted a reasonably simple style of construction and need not spend so much time at the fly-tying bench when I had rather be out on the stream.

The nymph dressings given below are a very short, simple series, from light to dark. They seem to cover my needs quite adequately and I seldom find it necessary to use other than these few patterns. The Collins nymphs and dressings will follow later in this chapter.

Number one:	Light nymph.
TAIL	Three strands from wood duck or mandarin side feather.
BODY	Natural seal's fur ribbed with narrow oval gold tinsel.
THORAX	First build up with some padding material such as cotton yarn or wool yarn. If the nymph is weighted, lead electric fuse wire is used as a foundation. This is wrapped over a base of lacquered tying silk while still wet, and gone over again with tying silk after it is wound on. This extra procedure is to keep the wire base from twisting on the hook. In the case of a weighted nymph, the fly can be reversed in the vise, and the thorax and wing cases put on what would ordinarily be the belly or

bottom of the nymph, as with a weighted fly, the hook will almost invariably turn point up in the water.

I doubt that it matters a great deal whether the wing cases are seen on top or bottom of the nymph when in the water. But if one fishes near the bottom, the more weedless position of the hook is an advantage, in which instance the wing cases should be shown in reverse position.

WING CASES   The wing cases in this particular nymph are suggested after the same dubbing of the body is wound over the thorax, by two tiny eyes of the jungle cock feather. These are tied in at the front and top of the thorax so that they project at a slight angle, one to each side.

HACKLE   European partridge, the more grayish feather.

HOOK SIZES   14, 12, 10.

Number two: Medium color nymph.

TAIL   Three short strands from the long tail feather of the cock pheasant (ringneck).

BODY   Hare's ear, tied rough and ribbed with narrow oval gold tinsel. After ribbing, the dubbing is picked out between the ribs with a dubbing needle to suggest the gills of the nymph and to add a softer outline.

THORAX   Same dubbing over padding or fuse wire. Before winding on this dubbing, the wing case feather is tied in at the back of the thorax, upside down and pointing to the tail of the fly.

WING CASES   Bright blue feather from wing of English kingfisher, lacquered when in place. This feather, although exactly what I need to suggest the sparkle of color or light on the wing cases, is apt to come apart after some use. I have tried to find a proper substitute and so far the best is a bit of synthetic silk floss, of the same or nearly the same color, heavily lacquered after tying in. It is permanent, but not as bright and sparkling as the feather.

My good friend, Harry Darbee, the fly-tier, recently suggested that the stripped quill from a large feather such as goose or swan could be dyed and used for this purpose. It should be much more nearly permanent than the rather delicate kingfisher feather, but as yet I have not had the opportunity of trying it out.

When the wing-case feather or silk has been tied in at the rear of the thorax, wind on the dubbing for the thorax and then bring the wing-case feather forward over the back (or belly, as the case may be) and tie in at the head.

HACKLE	European partridge, either the gray or brown speckled hackle feather. These partridge hackles are also a rather fragile feather, and the fibres are apt to break off quickly if roughly used. I have sometimes substituted a cree hackle for this nymph as well as others, and although I do not like the color and texture quite as well as the partridge, it seems to be about as effective.
HOOK SIZES	14, 12, 10, 8.

Number three:	Dark nymph.
TAIL	A few strands of dark cochy-bondhu or dark furnace hackle barbules.
BODY	Muskrat or mole fur mixed with red-brown dyed seal (same as both wet and dry fly bodies in other groups), ribbed with narrow oval gold tinsel. These nymph bodies should be rather loosely spun and tied rough, and the dubbing picked out between the ribs.
THORAX	Same as body.
WING CASES	Same as number two.
HACKLE	Dark furnace or cochy-bondhu hackle.
	In all these nymphs the hackle is clipped off top and bottom and just left at the sides.
HOOK SIZES	16, 14, 12, 10.

To these patterns I add a Tups Indispensable tied as a nymph. The dressing is the same as the variant given, but the hackle used is of conventional length rather than long, and clipped off at top and bottom.

If considerable weight is desired in the nymph—and this is sometimes a great asset—the fuse wire body is first wrapped over the entire length of the hook shank and the thorax built up over it. It is then gone over with the tying silk and lacquered before spinning on the body material.

When the body is completed, squeeze it gently between a pair of flat-nosed pliers to flatten it out in more nymph-like shape. If the fuse wire base is well lacquered this flat body will hold its shape very well.

There is another method of weighting nymph bodies, or those of any

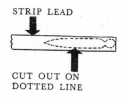

STRIP LEAD

CUT OUT ON
DOTTED LINE

BASE OF
TYING SILK

LEAD STRIP
TIED ON
SIDE VIEW

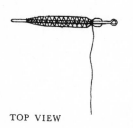

TOP VIEW

*Showing method
of weighting nymph
with strip-lead*

sunken fly, which is very effective. One of the advantages to this method of weighting is that the hook will not tend to turn upside down when submerged. The reason for this is that the weight is applied to the under-side of the hook (the side next to the point) rather than around the shank.

The procedure in tying is as follows: Procure some of the small lead "strip-matches" which come in little paper containers and which are ordinarily used to wrap around the leader to sink the fly or lure. With a scissors trim a strip of this lead into the shape shown in the illustration. Now wrap the hook shank with tying silk and lacquer it. Over the silk base tie in the lead strip as shown, *under* the hook shank. The soft lead will bend slightly to conform to the round shank and the small notch near the head of the fly will hold it from sliding down toward the bend of the hook. Over this lead base tie in the tail, spin and wrap on the dubbing as usual. All other processes are the same as usual except that the nymph thorax can be placed on top of the hook. The fly will ride hook point down in the water. This method of weighting was shown to me by Charles De Feo, a truly inventive fly-tier.

My own theories on the imitation of nymphs closely follow those on dry and wet flies—to try to approximate a group of naturals rather than to copy any particular one, and to employ the lifelike materials which lend the soft outline and impressionistic color effects.

COLLINS NYMPHS

For the angler who wishes to go in for the finer points of tying and fishing the nymph, I cannot recommend any patterns to compare with those given below. The group is very comprehensive in imitating the naturals found on our streams. The effect of these artificials in the water is amazingly lifelike, and in the soft-bodied type they carry out the theory of soft silhouette, and "sparkle" to a great degree.

Mr. Collins weights all of his patterns. However, the nymphs can be tied either with or without a fuse wire base, depending on conditions and the angler's preference. I personally believe the weighted type to be more effective on the whole, but there are occasions when the angler will wish to fish his nymph near the surface and then the unweighted style will be best.

Mr. Collins also prefers the hard-bodied type. My own experience has shown that the more impressionistic effect in the water is more successful. These differences of opinion are what make angling so fascinating, and it will only be proved to each angler whether one or the other is better by trying them himself.

The following list of materials will be necessary in tying the Collins hard-bodied nymphs:

1   Cotton embroidery floss, in as many shades of brown, green, yellow and gray as can be found, also black and white. As no one manufacturer makes all the useful shades, it will be a help to look over the notion departments of the large department stores. Of particular importance are the olive green and yellow shades. The following brands of mercerized cotton floss have been found satisfactory: D.M.C., Royal Society, Silkine Art Thread, Cynthia Pull Skein and Peri-Lusta.

2   Quick drying brushing lacquer in the following colors: Black, white, brown and yellow. Blending of these will produce all the necessary shades. (The lacquer called LACQ made by the Glidden Co., Cleveland, Ohio, is recommended.)

3   Fuse wire, in sizes from 1½ ampere up to 4 ampere.

4   Sapolin Metal Lacquer, number 105.

5   A pair of flat-jawed, long-nose pliers. The jaws should be at least ⅜ inch wide.

6   Transparent Duco Household Cement.

The tying instructions for the hard-bodied nymphs are as follows:

Step Number 1   With a hook in the vise, and starting near the eye, wrap down to the curve of the hook and back with an open criss-crossing of

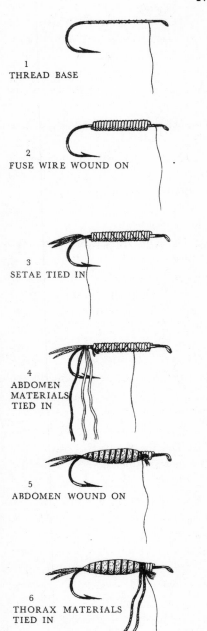

1
THREAD BASE

2
FUSE WIRE WOUND ON

3
SETAE TIED IN

4
ABDOMEN
MATERIALS
TIED IN

5
ABDOMEN WOUND ON

6
THORAX MATERIALS
TIED IN

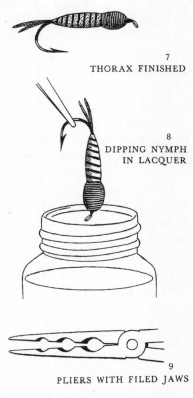

7
THORAX FINISHED

8
DIPPING NYMPH
IN LACQUER

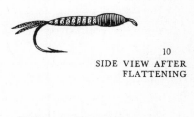

9
PLIERS WITH FILED JAWS

10
SIDE VIEW AFTER
FLATTENING

11
TOP VIEW AFTER
FLATTENING

Steps in tying Collins hard-bodied nymph

waxed thread, about size oo or ooo. This gives a foundation to prevent the body from turning on the hook shank in later operations.

Step Number 2   Tightly wind on the fuse wire over the thread base. Leave room at head and tail for tying in and tying off tails and body material. Pinch slightly with the pliers to tighten ends of wire. (For nymphs on number 14 hooks, use 1 or 2 ampere wire. For those on long shanked number 12 use 2 to 4 ampere wire.)

Step Number 3   Tie in setae or tails, either two or three, depending on type of nymph. These setae are usually the smallest natural hackle feathers found just back of the comb of the bird. By using hackles from the center and each side of the neck, the natural curve of the setae can be obtained.

Step Number 4   Tie in over the base of the tails, three strands of embroidery cotton of the proper color. The three strands will consist of two strands for the abdomen of one color, and one strand for ribbing of another color. Build up the abdomen and tie it off. Then wrap on ribbing and tie off. These are tied off at what will be the base of the thorax, or about one-third down the hook shank from the eye of the hook.

Step Number 5   Tie in thorax material. This is usually the same cotton floss as used for the body, but of another, darker color. Build up thorax larger than the abdomen. The thorax will cover the tied-off ends of the abdomen. Tie off thorax with whip-finish.

Step Number 6   With a pair of tweezers, grasp the nymph by the bend of the hook and immerse it in thin, clear lacquer up to the end of the abdomen. Hold it in the lacquer until it is entirely soaked. Then hang it up by the hook to dry. (The Sapolin Metal Lacquer number 105 is good for this step.) After the body has dried about an hour, squeeze it between the jaws of a pair of pliers to flatten it. The best pliers for this are prepared as follows: Take a pair of flat, long-nosed pliers and draw the temper by heat. When cool, file a flattened oval notch in the jaws as shown in the illustration. Two or three notches may be made to fit various sized nymph bodies. After shaping the bodies, soak them again in lacquer and hang them up to dry overnight.

Step Number 7   Take a medium sized hackle feather of the proper color from a soft, wet-fly neck. It should have plenty of web in it. Cut off the stiff points of the barbules, leaving the quill with the webby centers. Now place the nymph body on the table with the bend of the hook

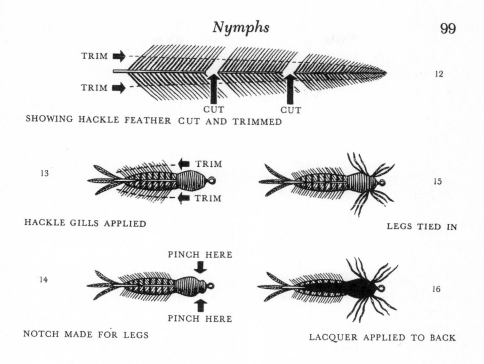

Steps in tying Collins hard-bodied nymph

upright. (As the Collins nymphs are rather heavily weighted, it is essential to tie them "upside down" or with the hook point on top.)

Cut out a section of the hackle feather the same length as the abdomen of the nymph. Cover the abdomen with Duco Household Cement, and with a pair of tweezers imbed the section of hackle in the cement. The cement dries immediately so that the hackle can then be trimmed off to suit the size of the nymph body. The webby barbules are to imitate the gills which occur along the sides of the abdomen. This hackle adds a great deal to the life-like effect of the nymph in the water.

Step Number 8   With a pair of thin-nosed pliers or some similar instrument, pinch grooves in the sides of the nymph thorax as shown. The grooves should be near the head. This notch is provided for tying in the legs and will tend to make the legs stand out away from the thorax. Mr. Collins uses fibres of the English partridge hackle feather for legs on most of his nymphs, and finds that they best imitate the legs of the natural. They are of a brown color with darker markings.

Tie in the legs with a few turns of tying silk. The legs should be

TRIM

STRIP ALL BARBULES FROM THIS SIDE

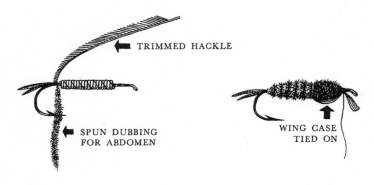

TRIMMED HACKLE

SPUN DUBBING
FOR ABDOMEN

WING CASE
TIED ON

LARGE HEAD

TRIM OFF HACKLE ON
TOP AND BOTTOM

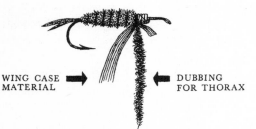

WING CASE
MATERIAL

DUBBING
FOR THORAX

FINISHED NYMPH
TOP VIEW

FINISHED NYMPH AFTER FLATTENING
AND AS IT RIDES IN THE WATER

Steps in tying Collins soft-bodied nymph

made of about four fibres on each side, with the heavy ends of the fibres next the eye of the hook. Tie in each set separately, one set on each side of the thorax. Trim off the fibres of feathers with a burning cigarette end, which results in a softer cut than when scissors are used.

Step Number 9   Paint the back of the nymph (this will be the top of the nymph when lying with the hook point upright) with the proper colored lacquer. In doing this operation, cover the entire back of the thorax but do not paint out to the edges of the abdomen. Just a stripe down the center so as to cover the center rib and part of the fibres of the hackle-gills. (See illustration.)

The wing cases may be suggested by painting the back of the thorax a darker color where desired. When lacquering the back of the thorax, allow some of the lacquer to touch the base of the legs where they are tied in. This will help to keep them at the proper angle to the thorax.

Some of the nymph dressings given below call for tails made of trimmed hackle ribs. These can be made by cutting away all of the hackle barbules from the center rib except a very narrow fringe down each side. The ribs are tied in in the usual manner.

The basis of the soft-bodied nymphs is one of softer materials and a resulting soft silhouette. Fur dubbing is used for bodies instead of cotton floss. The principle is much more in sympathy with my own theories of impressionism and the distinct, insect-like outline and coloration. The dubbing may be blended to obtain mixed colors and gold or silver ribbing used where desired.

Mr. Collins uses wool yarn as well as dubbing for the bodies as he finds it difficult to obtain furs of the proper color for certain patterns. However, dyed fur could be used, and the proper shade obtained by blending various colors together.

The procedure in tying the soft-bodied nymphs is as follows: Proceed the same as with hard-bodied nymphs for the first steps, or until the tails have been tied in.

Step Number 2   Prepare the fur or yarn for the abdomen. Take a soft webby hackle feather of the proper color for the gills of the nymph and prepare it as follows: Strip one side of the feather completely of all barbules. Then trim off the barbules on the other side, leaving only the short, webby fibres. Tie in the tip of this trimmed hackle, then the body material.

Step Number 3   Wind on dubbing or yarn to build up the abdomen, and tie off. Rib the abdomen with the trimmed hackle feather. Trim

off with scissors all hackle on top and bottom of the nymph, leaving
only that of the sides. This will represent the gills.

Step Number 4   Tie in thorax material and build up thorax by winding
this on. The thorax should cover the tie-off of the material used on
the abdomen. Leave enough room at eye of hook for legs.

If a wing case is desired on the nymph, the feather or other material
can be tied in at the same time with the thorax material, as described in
my own nymph patterns. Then when the thorax is wound on, the wing
case material can be brought forward and tied in at the head, over the
top of the thorax. Mr. Collins uses 8 or 10 fibres from the secondary
wing feather of the crow, black duck or mallard duck for these wing
cases. I personally prefer a more colorful material, with more sparkle.

Step Number 5   Prepare and tie in legs, in front of thorax. The bulge of
the thorax will hold the legs out at the base. By building up a rather
large head on the nymph, in front of the legs, this will tend to keep the
forward legs in proper position. English partridge is generally used for
legs in these nymphs, although occasionally Mr. Collins uses the fibres
of various wing feathers, separated and tied in.

Step Number 6   Flatten nymph with pliers.

List of hard-bodied nymphs used by Mr. Collins and their dressings:

Number 1:

TAILS	Three trimmed hackle points of dark ginger hackle.
ABDOMEN	Light olive green ribbed with light brown.
THORAX	Medium brown.
GILLS	Dark ginger hackle.
LEGS	English partridge.
BACK	Dark brown lacquer.
HOOK SIZES	14 or 14, 3x long.

Number 2:

TAILS	Three tiny reddish brown hackles.
ABDOMEN	A dirty, brownish yellow ribbed with light brown.
THORAX	Brown.
GILLS	Reddish brown hackle.
LEGS	English partridge.
BACK	Brown lacquer, with black over thorax.
HOOK SIZES	14, 3x long or 12 regular.

Number 3:

TAILS	Three tiny honey dun hackles, or light buff hackles.
ABDOMEN	Palest yellow ribbed with white, or use white ribbed with yellow.
THORAX	Light tan or yellowish tan.
GILLS	Honey dun hackle.
LEGS	English partridge.
BACK	Light brown lacquer.
HOOK SIZES	12, 3x long or 12 regular.

Number 4:

TAILS	Three tiny mahogany red hackles.
ABDOMEN	Reddish brown or purplish red ribbed with dark brown.
THORAX	Dark brown.
GILLS	Mahogany red hackle.
LEGS	English partridge.
BACK	Dark brown.
HOOK SIZES	12, 3x long.

Number 5:

TAILS	Three tiny rusty dun hackles.
ABDOMEN	Grayish, dirty yellow, ribbed with medium gray.
THORAX	Grayish brown.
GILLS	Rusty dun hackle.
LEGS	English partridge.
BACK	Light grayish brown over abdomen. Brown over thorax.
HOOK SIZES	12, 3x long.

Number 6:

TAILS	Three tiny black hackles.
ABDOMEN	Medium gray, ribbed with fine oval tinsel.
THORAX	Dark gray or dark brown.
GILLS	Black hackle.
LEGS	English partridge.
BACK	Dark gray over abdomen. Black over thorax.
HOOK SIZES	14, or 12, 3x long.

Soft bodied nymphs and dressings:

Number 1:

TAILS	Three points of trimmed ginger hackles.
ABDOMEN	Muskrat mixed with dyed red mole fur or red cashmere yarn, to get a reddish-gray color. Ribbed with trimmed ginger hackle for gills.
THORAX	Medium brown or dark mole. Paint the top of the thorax with grayish-brown lacquer to give it a hard, humped appearance.
LEGS	English partridge.
HOOK SIZES	14 or 10.

Number 2:

TAILS	Three tiny light brown hackles.
ABDOMEN	Red fox belly or amber colored mole fur. Ribbed with trimmed light brown hackle for gills.
THORAX	Dark brown mole or beaver.
LEGS	English partridge.
HOOK SIZES	12, 3x long.

Number 3:

TAILS	Three tiny rusty dun hackles, tied in short, $\frac{1}{8}$ to $\frac{1}{4}$ inch beyond bend of hook.
ABDOMEN	Claret-colored yarn mixed with dark-brown mole or beaver, to get a reddish-brown color. Ribbed with trimmed rusty dun hackle for gills.
THORAX	Black fur or yarn mixed with dark brown.
LEGS	English partridge.
HOOK SIZES	12, 3x long or 10 regular.

Number 4:

TAILS	Three tiny rusty dun or blue dun hackles.
ABDOMEN	Light green yarn, shredded and mixed with gray muskrat fur to get a greenish gray color. Ribbed with trimmed dun hackle for gills.
THORAX	Dark gray fur or yarn.
LEGS	English partridge.
HOOK SIZES	14, 3x long or 14 regular.

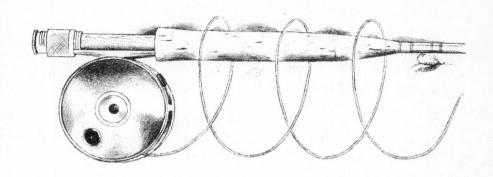

CHAPTER XII   *Touching on Rods*

THERE HAS been a decided tendency in recent years toward rods which are stiffer and faster in action that those of the past. To a great extent this is a good thing, as the rods of twenty or thirty years ago were apt to be too slow and soft. But as frequently is the case, a movement away from one tendency has swung too far in the opposite direction. With the advent of the stiffer rod, lines necessarily have had to be increased in weight. Too often the angler has become a sort of tournament caster on the stream, constantly trying for greater distance and experimenting with various rod and line combinations to achieve it. Almost invariably, when discussing rods and lines with an angler of this type, I am impressed with the fact that he is more concerned with casting than he is with fishing. Of course, casting in itself can be a lot of fun, but when it becomes more important than fishing—the correct and successful presentation of the fly, the hooking of the fish, and the pleasure given the angler in use of the rod—the means unfortunately becomes the end.

I believe one could safely wager that the average trout is taken with a cast no longer than forty feet. Except in a river of very large size, the long-casting angler is probably using more line than he should instead of trying to find a position nearer the fish. Sometimes, in very flat, still water, it is necessary to throw a considerable distance but even here a great deal can be accomplished by the angler rather than the rod. It is not only much harder to present the fly properly at long distances, but is also more difficult to hook the fish if he does rise.

Heavy lines are harder to float and much more noticeable to the fish. They make the delicate presentation, so necessary in difficult conditions, a serious problem. In a large, rough stream, like a steelhead river, I doubt if any of these arguments carries much weight. But as many of us are concerned with conditions where we must use every caution to achieve success, I believe we could profit by more delicate tackle.

I constantly hear complaints from tired anglers who spend a great deal of time resting their wrists from the demands of a stiff rod. And strangely enough they are convinced that their outfit calls for less effort on their part. They claim that the rod does the work. That is quite true, but why, then, are there tired muscles?

The ideal compromise between a too stiff and a too soft rod is one which handles well a line light enough for delicate fishing but heavy enough to achieve respectable distance. It should feel light in the hand, not top-heavy, and it should not tire the angler. A large part of our fishing, at least in the East, is done with a rod of about eight feet, weighing in the neighborhood of four ounces. This rod, if stiff and fast, usually calls for a line of about .050 inch or C in the heavy portion, whether torpedo head or double taper. I believe a C line is too much line for easy, delicate fishing. I have seen eight-foot rods with which one could cast properly only by using a line of at least .055 inch or B—tackle I would avoid instinctively for any trout fishing.

My own favorites, which seem to me to embrace the qualities so necessary for enjoyable and efficient casting and fishing, are two rods very similar in action. They are each eight feet long. One, a Leonard of many years' use, weighs four ounces, a tournament type, so called. It is powerful for its weight and will cast amazing distances, but its action is not too fast and can be felt well down into the butt. If held firmly in two hands and slowly "waggled" in a horizontal plane so that the tip describes an arc of about three feet, the action starts in the butt about nine inches above the handgrasp.

The line used on this rod is a silk line of about .041 or .042 inch, a little large for E. It also handles very well a size D or .045 inch in nylon. These lines are torpedo lines, but made to the specification of Edward Hewitt, with a much longer belly so that, unless one is casting a long line, it is very much like a conventional double taper. Somehow this combination of rod and line has given me more real satisfaction than any other I ever used, with the exception of my second favorite. One does not need the powerful wrist snap to propel a line with these rods. It can be a slow swing, as when using a wet fly on still water or when a delicate delivery is essential. The rod dries the fly with only the slightest wrist motion and when called upon to reach out, will pick up and shoot a tremendous amount of line.

The other favorite is a Gillum, eight feet and about three and seven-eighths ounces. Although a trifle lighter in weight than the Leonard, the Gillum is slightly stiffer and shows the action, when waggled, down to about twelve inches above the handgrasp. Otherwise, the two rods are very nearly identical in action and I use the same lines for both. At the present time I am confined to the Gillum rod, for after lending the Leonard to my wife some years ago, she appropriated it to the extent of practically full ownership and I am rarely able to "borrow" it for a day on the river.

The Gillum rod is of cane that has not been heated other than for the necessary straightening. This tends to give a slightly slower action than when heat has been applied to harden and color the bamboo. The Leonard rod is of natural-colored cane. I understand that some heat is used in the preparation of the Leonard rods. But these rods have never seemed to me to have the quick action of those in which the cane has been strongly colored by greater heat on the surface.

It seems that heat-treated cane is much more in demand for rods at present, due, no doubt, to its increased speed of action. However, for me the action of untreated or lightly treated cane is more pleasant. Apparently cane which is treated with heat is faster and more powerful for the same weight. But the type of power is of a different sort, and I personally prefer my lighter rods to be made of cane which has the slightly slower, smoother "feel."

If bamboo is overheated it becomes brittle, resulting in danger of breakage and a shorter life.

I am still somewhat in doubt about the results of the intensive baking necessary for impregnation of cane with plastics. This new rod-building technique, however, does offer several great improvements. The joined cane can be soaked in water for great lengths of time with no ill results and has even been boiled, in certain tests which I have heard of, without loosening the bond. No varnish is necessary which is undoubtedly a great advantage. The finish is particularly beautiful to look at and is quite permanent.

There is also another point regarding the plastic-impregnated rod which was brought out by a good friend who is a rod maker. He stated that in use, and particularly during very warm weather, the friction generated by movement of the cane has a tendency to soften the glue in the conventional rod where animal glue is used as a bond. This results in a certain slowness of action beyond that which is desirable, and over periods of time can cause a permanent slowing down of the rod. As the conventional hide glues are heated to only about 130 degrees or 150 degrees Fahrenheit in joining the strips of cane, this is barely possible. But with the plastic bonds, heated to around 300 degrees, the claim is that no heat from air temperature or friction can alter the consistency of the bonds. In other words, the rod joined with a plastic is more apt to retain its "snap" in all conditions.

My own natural reactions to this argument as well as that of some of my angling friends is that such generation of heat will need to be proved. The great secret of the resiliency of cane is that the longitudinal fibres are bound firmly in place and do not move relatively. The flexion of any material can generate heat, but the generation of even one degree of heat by the ordinary flexion of a fishing rod must be proved by actual tests with a thermometer before it is credible.

In considering the relative efficiency of plastic bonds versus animal glue, one must take into consideration the flexibility of the latter. At present, this seems to be the best argument in favor of animal glues and the one weakness of synthetic cements or plastic glues. Also, the one great weakness of animal glue, of course, is its vulnerability to moisture. It will remain to be seen how modern rodmakers will work out this problem. I am convinced that at least there are great possibilities in the use of modern plastics as a bond for the strips of cane.

The more powerful rods of my own—those used for steelhead or salmon fishing—are of heat-treated cane. When casting a dry fly for salmon, the lighter rods are certainly an advantage, as they do not tire the angler so readily, and can take a lighter line which is an advantage in low water. The rods I have of eight and one-half feet or nine feet are sufficiently powerful for all the distance I need, yet, even with their added power, they weigh no more than the natural cane rods of the same length.

In touching so lightly upon such an extremely controversial subject as rod construction, heat treatment of cane and its plastic impregnation, I realize that I may do no more than stimulate the reader to inquire further into this very interesting branch of angling.

There is much to be learned about rod making, particularly about bonds for the strips of cane. My own knowledge of rod building mechanics is slight, but I believe that the angler should have at least a smattering of the important facts relevant to rod construction.

Some rodmakers recently have developed the "hollow-butt" rod, which seems to offer interesting possibilities. It is claimed that these rods give greater lightness with increased speed and still adequate strength.

While in the West recently I looked at several of these rods and, although I tried only one, a nine-foot model, they seemed to have fine qualities. In tournament work they have undoubtedly proved their worth, but the rods which have broken the records are hardly what one would call fishing rods, being built primarily for one purpose, that of achieving distance. The rods I tried were owned by Peter J. Schwab and, although I did not agree with many of his theories concerning rods and lines for fishing, I was captivated by several very small, light rods he showed me. He called them "leetle fellers." They were of seven feet and only slightly over two ounces, made by Stoner of the Winston Rod Company. Mr. Schwab, or Pete, as we all call him, uses the little rods almost exclusively for stream trout fishing and claims that they do everything that the larger ones will do. They are said to handle enough line to place the fly farther than he can see it properly, which is certainly far enough for anyone, and to have great mobility. "It is just like pointing your finger to fish with one of these," Pete says. With them he uses a small torpedo head line of his own design.

When conditions justify it I, too, like the little rods and have a beautiful seven-foot Gillum which is very light. With an E line, it becomes a lovely combination to cast with. But I don't attempt to fish a large river with it, or use it when I have to face a strong wind. It is ideal for low-water conditions where one can wade and get in position for a difficult fish, or on medium and small streams.

In naming certain rods and their makers, I realize that I have "stuck my neck out." It is hardly fair to name some without including the whole list of those whose rods can be included in the "first rate" category. I can only say that in naming certain rods of mine I have stated a personal preference. Every angler knows that it is possible to go through a large number of rods before finding one the action of which suits him perfectly. The favorite Leonard I spoke of was the result of a critical examination of every eight-foot rod at William Mills & Son in New York City, not only by myself but by two very experienced angling friends.

During the years spent on trout streams I have used a great number of different rods, by different makers. One of the best I ever owned was a Granger (made by the original company), costing twelve dollars. This ancient tool is still in use after almost thirty years. Another favorite is a

Payne, which has been responsible for many thousands of casts and a considerable number of trout. It is as straight and casts as well as the day it came out of the shop.

Garrison is another excellent rod designer and builder. His rods show the test of time and use. The new plastic-bonded and -impregnated rods produced by Orvis, a near neighbor in Vermont, are excellent. They have greatly improved their design and workmanship over earlier models and have acquired many enthusiastic users.

These rods are the ones I am familiar with and which I know have proved their excellence, but that does not mean that they are the only ones. Every angler has his own favorites and he will undoubtedly find the one rod, at some time in his career, which is best for him.

Whether or not we agee with the English anglers in their choice of rods, we must admit that with their fishing, the winds so constantly present on English streams, and the necessity of casting from the bank rather than from the water, an entirely different type of weapon is called for. Rather than condemn it all as useless in America, we should profit by some of their discoveries. There are occasions here when the longer, softer rods might be an advantage. Wherever the delivery should be very delicate, or where a long, light cast is essential, our short powerful rods are sometimes unable to give us what we want. And particularly if one fishes where wind is a governing factor, it can be very discouraging to try to achieve the proper results with a rod unsuitable and inadequate for the job.

Of course, for the man who can afford a large battery of rods of every length, weight and description, it is not difficult to find something to take care of the unusual condition. But for the one- or two-rod man, it is something else again. If I could only have one rod for trout, it would be either eight feet three inches or eight and one-half feet, of medium, not stiff action, to handle a line not over size D in silk or nylon. This would enable one to fish delicately if desired, cover large water, handle a wind, or fish a short line. And I would ask "Pinky" Gillum to make it for me.

Once my wife was given a rod as a present, and as it did not suit her, being too stiff and powerful, she sent it to the maker with the request that he try to find something more appropriate to her needs. The maker, who was Powell, of California, returned a rod which was a combination of rods and, as it worked out, was very useful and practical. He wrote that in making up a nine-foot model of the desired action, it occurred to him to try a shorter butt section, one which brought the length down to eight and one-half feet. This made such a grand rod that he sent along both butts, with no extra charge. As a result the short butt is nearly always used, although the rod can be quickly made into a nine-footer by shifting to the long butt. The combination is one of great utility. Needless to say, we appreciated the thought and generosity of the rod maker.

At present there seems to be less of a tendency to differentiate between rods for wet-fly and those for dry-fly fishing, which is as it should be. There seems to be no logical reason for changing rods when changing flies unless the water or some other outside factor enters into the problem. Actually, what should decide the choice of rod is how one wishes to present the fly. Whether the fly be on or below the water doesn't matter. In fishing flat, smooth water, particularly if low and clear, it seems more sensible to employ rods and tackle suitable for very delicate casting. In this case I would use a rod on the softer side which would handle a finer line and longer leader than one employed for working over fast, broken water where the casts are short and frequent and a faster rod with heavier line for the short delivery is an advantage.

As soon as one enters the big water, where it is essential to produce distance, it does not seem important to me whether wet or dry fly will be used, but whether the rod will handle the line necessary and fish the fly properly. Another factor which has a definite bearing on the choice of rod is the weight of leader used. If very fine gut is essential, the rod should certainly be fine enough and soft enough in the tip to avoid breakage of the leader when striking. In nymph fishing, which requires the finest gut to achieve a freely moving fly in the water, the most delicate rod action is called for. But in using a large wet fly or streamer where big fish might be encountered, a fairly powerful rod would be more suitable.

CHAPTER XIII   *Lines and Leaders*

It is essential that the angler find the right line for the rod to balance properly his fly-fishing outfit. If he hasn't the proper combination of line and rod, casting is not pleasant or effective, and frequently he may be unaware of what is causing the trouble. Some tackle dealers maintain facilities for trying out different lines by actual casting, but outside of a few dealers in the large cities, anglers will find that the only solution is to buy a line and hope that it will work.

Without the preliminary try-out, choice may be pretty much a matter of buying a pig in a poke, and anglers are apt to continue using a poorly balanced outfit for want of some way of improving it.

It is possible to approximate closely the tapers of a line, and obtain any proportions desired, by splicing together lengths of level lines of various sizes. The taper on machine-made lines is produced by cutting one thread at a time, at regular intervals, so that after each cut there is one less thread in the braid. It is really a close series of micrometrically fine level steps, varying about .001 inch more or less. The fisherman cannot get such fine variations; he has to use pieces of standard level lines, which vary by about .005 inch between sizes, although careful measurement of a lot of different lines nominally the same size will produce interesting and useful variations.

It is not difficult to splice one's own lines to suit the rod, and this is one of the few practical solutions that I know of for the troubles one has in matching the two. When anglers build their own tapers it is an easy matter to make changes until the line casts well and straightens out as it should. There is no reason why a properly spliced line should ever break at the point of juncture or become weakened with even considerable use. I have subjected spliced lines to very rough and lengthy treatment with no suggestion of trouble.

If the angler is wedded to the conventional double-tapered line, there isn't much that can be done by splicing, other than shortening or lengthening the tapers. But this type of line can be greatly improved, in my estimation, by other alterations that will result in a modified torpedo head, which is much more useful and practical for average fishing.

It might be well here to define the terms used in denoting the various parts of a line. Beginning at the "point," which is the end to be attached to the leader, there is a section of level line which varies in length from a few feet to as much as six or eight. It is ordinarily the smallest diameter of the line. This is intended to be shortened by the angler to suit his rod or his type of casting and fishing.

I have never found the need for more than a foot or two of this level line at the most. I generally cut it off at the beginning of the front taper, which is the part of the line next above the "point." This front taper, which will be the same at both ends of the standard double-tapered line, varies in length according to the maker or the type of line. It may be as short as six or eight feet, and it is sometimes as long as twelve or fifteen. After the front taper comes the belly, or heavy part of the line. In the standard double taper, this continues to the back taper as a level line. In the torpedo types it can vary in diameter and length considerably and is always the heaviest part of the line.

Moving backward, on the torpedo line, comes a short section which tapers down to a smaller diameter again. This is called the back-taper, and in some cases the pick-up line. This section then joins the long level running or shooting line, which continues to the reel or backing. The backing is usually a piece of small bait-casting or spinning line of a length required by the type of fishing to be done and spliced or looped to the running line.

The purpose of the torpedo type line is to get out, on a short cast, sufficient weight to make the rod work, and to permit casts a great deal longer without overloading the rod. With the weight concentrated in a small part of the front of the line, it makes possible greater shooting power with no more actual weight.

The type of fishing done will decide the tapers of lines, and anglers should hardly employ an extreme torpedo with a heavy belly for use in delicate dry-fly fishing on low, clear water. And they could not expect to achieve the distances essential to fish properly a big salmon or steelhead river with a light, double-tapered line, even though the line might suit the rod.

The same rod can work well with a combination of lines. It might handle a torpedo of about .050 inch in the belly for the distance work and at the same time make a good combination with a standard or slightly modified double taper of around .045 inch which would be more suitable for delicate fishing.

It is essential to consider the uses to which the line will be put before designing it. A line that will float is needed for dry-fly fishing. There is nothing so irritating as a heavy, soggy line when the angler wants it on the surface for clean pickups and a high-riding fly. The smaller the line diameter, the better it will float. It is the surface tension, the "skin" on the water, that floats a line. We have all seen the experiment in which a cambric needle is made to float on the invisible skin of the water. But did you ever see a darning needle float similarly? Both needles have the same specific gravity—weight relative to volume—but a large needle has much less surface proportionately than a small one. The small needle is nearly all surface.

If one takes lines of identical manufacture but ranging in size from A to H, he will find that H floats best; that between E and C, the largest size does not float as nicely as the smaller; that B is a poor floater and that A can scarcely be made to float at all. All have the same specific gravity, the same finish, but different ratios of weight to surface exposed.

Naturally, knowing that this is true, the angler would avoid a large-diametered line for dry-fly work. The same might be said of a line to be used for wet fly as well, as long as the fishing to be done is of the delicate sort. The wet line is proportionately heavier in use, due to the weight of water it soaks up, and the angler might even use a lighter line for this fishing. My own preference is always for light rather than heavy lines as it makes for effective fishing and less fuss in the water. As a rule my

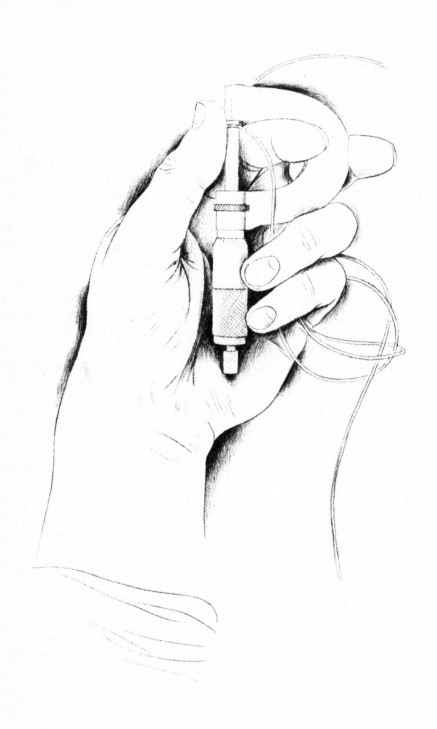

equipment contains more lines than rods, and the combination is chosen more for efficient fishing than for actual casting. I believe that there is a tendency toward the use of lines heavier than necessary, due to the fact that one can easily cast a longer line with them, and that frequently one is apt to use more line than necessary in his fishing.

To make the proper combinations of tapers in a line, it is essential to have some sort of micrometer to determine dimensions accurately. Here again my good friend "Sparse Gray Hackle" comes to my assistance with some excellent advice. The suggestions following are due greatly to his much greater knowledge of mechanics.

It is not only possible to get any desired measurements from a line by screwing the micrometer down harder and harder; it seems to be the habit of a great many anglers in measuring diameters. It is important that one use the same "squeeze" every time he takes a measurement. That will give at least a comparative accuracy. A good idea would be to start by setting the zero on the micrometer at the point where "he can feel the anvils come together" and several tries are not too many to check that setting. Next, in measuring, one should approximate the same "hand."

Try sliding the line between the anvils a short distance—as line dimensions vary considerably from end to end—and keep loosening the micrometer. Keep the line straight, not bent, and work it back and forth gently and repeatedly to get the hand.

Taper gauges are practically worthless for this work as one can get almost any dimensions he desires. A simple and practical help is to collect short samples of lines in graduated sizes and known to be accurate. Hang them side by side so that comparison by touch with one after another can readily be made. The hand is surprisingly accurate and can be trained to be even more so.

Probably the most useful combination of tapers in a line can be made by altering a conventional double taper. This is the type of line which I use most. It is excellent in the smaller sizes for all delicate fishing and has an advantage over the original tapers in that distance can be achieved with less strain on the rod. Longer shoots are much easier. Any double-tapered line also has the advantage of being reversible if used in its original form. Or two modified torpedo head lines may be made from the single double taper. This offers considerable saving to the angler as most lines now are on the costly side.

In the following descriptions of line design and splicing, this table of line sizes will eliminate repetition of measurements in both letters and thousands of an inch. For all practical purposes these sizes are standard:

Size H=.025 inch   Size D=.045 inch
Size G=.030 inch   Size C=.050 inch
Size F =.035 inch   Size B=.055 inch
Size E=.040 inch   Size A=.060 inch

A trout rod of average or medium action eight feet in length would call for a line similar to the following: Take a silk line of standard double taper, size HDH, and cut off the point to within two feet of the beginning of the front taper. (The taper should be as short as possible in choosing a line of this type.) Measuring from this end, cut the line off at a total length of thirty-three feet. To this end splice on a three-foot length of E line, and to that splice the running line of F. The latter can be left its original 25-yard length which will give a total over-all length of line of 111 feet. Or the running line can be shortened to make the total around ninety feet, giving more room on the reel for backing.

With a nine-foot leader, the cast will be forty-five feet before running line is needed. This is a good distance for pick-up in a long cast, and as most of our fishing is done at even closer range, it will seldom be necessary to use the running line at all. Actually, we will be fishing with what corresponds to a standard double tapered line until we wish to cast over forty-five feet. Then with the running line coming into use, the rod strain is not increased, and our longer shoots are made more easily.

Size F running line seems to me the best for nearly all the torpedo combinations. If smaller than this, it has a tendency to twist or kink when loops are held in the hand and can be damaged easily. Unless using a light rod and a line with a belly of E, I would never go smaller. In the latter combination, it might be advisable to reduce the running line to G.

One alteration may be necessary to the combination described above. That is, it may be better to reduce the point of the line to the actual beginning of the front taper. If one finds that the line and leader do not straighten out sufficiently or that this straightening is late in coming, reducing the point probably will correct it. This will cut the length of the torpedo section to 43 feet, but will make no appreciable difference in the weight.

The proportions given above are only suggested as one solution, and are not to be taken as the ideal combination by any means. The line described works well for me, but slight differences in rod action or casting technique may make it necessary to alter these proportions. The principal reason for splicing lines is to arrive at the best combination for the angler and the fishing he will do, and one may experiment with taper designs until the correct one is found.

The more extreme torpedo tapers offer even greater opportunities for experimentation. These lines, in the heavier weights, are generally used for distance work on large waters. Where the angler fishes with a rod of 8½ or 9 feet and wants to be able to handle a long line for steelhead or salmon, the spliced combinations offer excellent possibilities. I had rather obtain a torpedo line in the beginning with which to experiment and it might be that the ideal combination will be found at once so that no splicing is necessary. Unfortunately, I have yet to find the exact combination for my own requirements, and in every case have had to alter it slightly.

If I were to try out a new torpedo line, I would first determine, if possible, how much of the level point should be removed. In almost every case in my experience the line has been improved by cutting this off entirely, but it should be done gradually, with trials in between, to be sure. I like to leave a few extra inches which will, in time, be used up as the point of the line wears away.

If the line appears to be too light for the rod, I would suggest splicing a piece of line of the next size larger than the belly into the rear part of the belly, next to the back-taper. If the belly is, say, twenty feet long, try splicing in six to eight feet of the next larger size, without removing a corresponding section of the belly. This will lengthen the belly, of course, and may make it too heavy, as well as too long. If you wish only slight added weight, it would be best to remove a corresponding section of line where the new one is spliced in, retaining the original length but increasing the weight.

As it is necessary to consider the type of casting or fishing to be done with any line in order to explain thoroughly the reasons for its design, I am taking it for granted that your own decisions will be based on your requirements. The line just described, for example, is one used more for distance work than otherwise. If it were for short casts where power was essential, I would advise the added weight in the belly to be spliced in at the front, rather than the rear. But for distance work, the heavier rear belly seems to be best, at least for me.

One of the objections which anglers frequently offer is that torpedo lines do not roll-cast well and are difficult to mend, or to use for throwing loops or slack with a long line.

The line first described, with longer belly than usual, will be found more practical for such uses. In fact, wherever the angler does considerable roll-casting or mending of the line, I would certainly advise the use of a longer belly. The diameter can be reduced if the greater length adds too much weight. It is the *weight* of the line, in each case, which decides its efficiency in casting. This means that designs should be governed by a process of selection and balance to obtain that weight where it is most needed.

In the West there is a tendency among anglers to go in for distance casting in a big way. Naturally, the size of the rivers in many places makes this essential if they hope to cover the water. There also seems to be more interest there in tournament casting and anglers are apt to experiment with tackle in search of added length of cast. Some of these casters have begun to use nylon monofilament, or leader material, for running line, and, although I have not actually seen it done, I have heard of incredible distances made with such tackle. It seems to me that it would be unsuited for fishing, however, due to its greater stiffness. The consequence of a loop caught around a finger, should a heavy fish strike at that moment, might well be serious. I saw such wounds on the hands of a man I met there, but when I questioned him about it, he seemed not to mind the risk of injury if he could thereby add twenty or thirty feet to his cast.

In building a splice in a line, I have found a certain type to be best, and have never had it give way or cause trouble in casting. Any splice will wear, in time, and eventually will need replacement, but it takes a lot of casting to wear it down. The most important factor is the length, which should not be over five-eighths of an inch at the most. One-half inch is better. This is adequate for strength and it will shoot through the guides more easily. Also it will tend to stiffen the line less at that point than if it were longer.

I begin by lightly scraping the finish from the ends of the line sections to be spliced together and then, with a dubbing needle, pick apart the strands for one-fourth or three-eighths of an inch so that they are well unraveled. When both ends are so prepared, I divide each into two parts, as illustrated in the diagram, and with a small pair of scissors trim away the strands to a blunt point. Do not cut away too much or the splice will be weakened, but only enough so that it will taper gradually from each

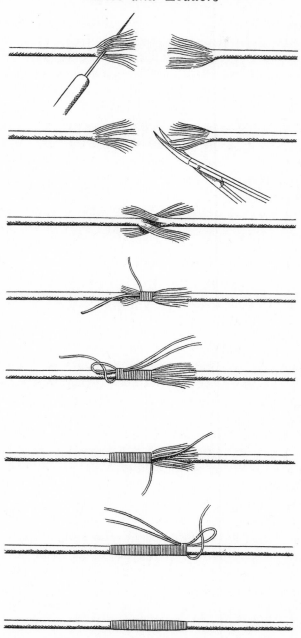

Steps in splicing line

end. The ends are crossed over, as shown, and a wrapping of silk thread begun in the middle, working toward one end. Well waxed silk helps, and I use 2/o for this stage. When the winding has reached a point about one-fourth inch from the center, tie in a pull-through, as in wrapping a rod, and pull the end of the silk back under a few turns to hold it fast. Begin again in the middle and wrap toward the other end in the same manner. It helps to have one end of the section of line fastened to something solid, so that it can be held taut with the left hand while wrapping with the right. Enough pressure should be used to insure a good, tight bond. If desired, the ends of the line may be touched with a bit of lacquer before wrapping, but I think this unnecessary.

After completing the wrapping, give it a thin coat of lacquer. When this is dry, or, better, when it is still slightly tacky, put the line on a smooth surface and *roll* the spliced section under a flat, smooth object such as a ruler, which will make it round and smooth. Now cover the entire splice with another wrapping of very fine silk; I use 6/o fly-tying silk for this but 4/o is fine enough. Extend the new wrapping very slightly beyond the heavier one so as to properly taper the splice, and, when finished, lacquer and roll it again. When this is dry, I give mine two coats of thin rod varnish or spar varnish.

If experimenting on tapers, it is not necessary to finish each splice completely before trying the line; in fact it would overdo an ordinarily interesting job. When the line is found suitable, the final wrappings and varnishings can be applied. It is a good idea, at the same time, to splice a small loop of one-half an inch in the end of the line to which the leader is attached. A neat, streamlined loop will help considerably to eliminate fuss in the water at the point of juncture. To aid in changing lines from one reel to another, without the necessity of a new splice to the backing each time this is done, one may also splice another small loop in the reel end of the line. Then splice a loop in the end of the backing large enough to admit the reel. The two loops may be fastened by placing one over the other and passing the reel through the larger loop.

When a line becomes worn and roughened by use, it can be renovated to a certain extent by a little judicious refinishing if the silk or nylon fibres are not damaged. I would not recommend trying to work over a line which is too far gone, or one which has become sticky. This seems to me to be a job for the maker and he will refinish a line so that it is almost like new. (At present it is doubtful whether more than one or two line makers will undertake this job.) But for the average line which has lost some of its finish, it can be improved so as to cast and fish better, and will last longer. I always hate to discard a good line that has served me well. It takes time to break a new one in so that it has that nice pliability without being too soft.

Recently, I did a small repair job on an old line. I stretched it out between some wooden pegs and rubbed it with a cloth soaked in pure boiled linseed oil touched with powdered pumice. This smoothed up the rough spots and reduced the old finish slightly. I then cleaned it well with the linseed oil and let it dry for several days. Then I applied another coat of the oil to which had been added a small proportion of Valspar varnish (about ten percent), and allowed this to dry again. The varnish quickens the drying rate, and adds smoothness to the finish but one should avoid the glassy, hard finish which accompanies the use of two much varnish. If this finish is applied with a cloth, it is almost impossible to make the coating too heavy. The resulting thin dressing dries beautifully. The line now has a smoother, harder finish, without any appreciably greater stiffness. It should last another season or two.

Some anglers use very fine steel wool for rubbing down a line, but this should be done cautiously as it cuts the finish quickly and reduces the diameter.

The proper combination of rod and line is not complete until balanced with a good leader. It is surprising how much a poorly tapered leader can affect the casting, and this trouble is frequently due to the gut being too light next to the line. A great many commercially tied leaders in lengths up to twelve feet have gut no larger than .012 inch or .013 inch at the heavy end. If one can handle these dimensions properly, it is an advantage to have fine gut throughout the length. But I have never been able to cast well with anything under .015 inch to .017 inch for the butt or top of a leader of nine feet or over. If the line is very fine at the point, it calls for light gut, but we rarely see dimensions which do not require a fairly large leader diameter. Some of my long leaders, twelve to fourteen feet, are made with tops of around .019 inch, particularly for use on a heavier line such as we employ for salmon or steelhead. Natural silkworm gut is difficult to obtain in good quality in these large diameters, but it can be used for a long time if examined regularly and retied when it shows signs of wear.

The development of nylon leader material has been a great boon, coming as it did when good silkworm gut was almost unobtainable. For general work it greatly simplifies fishing and the angler is sure of a reasonably even standard of quality. Most of the silkworm gut I used came from England, and necessitated a certain amount of trouble and delay in obtaining it. Now one may drop into a shop almost anywhere and buy the nylon material in a variety of weights that will handle a large proportion of our fishing.

I had rather use silkworm gut of good quality for dry-fly trout fishing, but have adopted nylon for dry-fly salmon fishing and all occasions where it is not important to use the smaller diameters. Tapered leaders of nylon are easily tied and one may, by experimenting, work out the best tapers for his particular needs. For such heavy work as bucktail or streamer fishing, it is even possible simply to unroll a sufficient quantity and cut off what is needed, making a knotless level leader.

The Hewitt silver nitrate stain, used on silkworm gut to eliminate flash, has always been my preference for really exacting work and I have been amazed at how long some of this material has lasted. It has slightly more strength per diameter than untreated gut and, according to some authorities who have kept accurate records of percentage of rises, accounts for a definitely higher proportion than mist-colored or natural-colored gut. There is no doubt that it is actually more visible in the water. I have never felt that the sight of gut itself is what causes fish to refuse the fly, but its magnified reflection or the shadow it casts when floating. Actually, trout are accustomed to seeing things in the water which are similar in appearance to the leader, such as grasses or weeds, and they do not necessarily connect such appearances with danger unless these objects act in an unusual manner.

The reason for fine gut in the leader is actually to give the fly more freedom of movement—to allow it to be unhampered and thus more lifelike to the trout. With the softer attachment, the currents may move the fly as they would the natural insect. Especially in nymph fishing, the delicate response to every change of current makes a much more lifelike presentation. Any suggestion of unnatural movement frightens fish most of all. That is why the drag of a dry fly is so apt to put them down.

Nylon doesn't seem to need the careful treatment of gut to preserve it properly, but there is no doubt that the life of silkworm gut can be lengthened a great deal by a degree of care. Nearly everyone agrees that the best method of preserving leaders is to keep them moist throughout the season, once they have been soaked, rather than alternately drying and soaking them as they are used. My own ,method is to soak my felt pads in a fifty percent solution of ethylene glycol in water which keeps leaders soft and flexible and prolongs their life. A saturated solution of soda may be added to keep the pads sweet, but I rarely use this myself. All leaders not in use should be kept out of the light and brought out only when needed.

I have used leaders, kept in this manner, for several years by retying them where needed and using new strands of gut on the point. But my good friend "Sparse Gray Hackle," (whose hackles, by the way, are hardly as sparse as those of your correspondent!) is determined not to lose a good fish or a favorite fly by risking old gut, and describes his methods as to how to treat it as follows: "At the end of the season, while my heart is strong and next year is far away, I open my soaking pouch and remove therefrom every vestige of leaders and points—including, dammit, the several leaders I had to soak up and put in service right at the end of the season. I toss, hurl, throw, launch, pitch, bowl and otherwise propel said gut just as far from me as possible, into the bushes. Then I walk rapidly away. I can think of no more horrible revenge on an enemy than to give him last year's leaders!" Then he adds further, "Of course I am not speaking for anyone who defies the laws of nature like————, who leaves leaders on strung-up rods all summer exposed to ultra-violet light; goes down to fish and starts casting with a spinner on a perfectly dry leader; socks the iron into any fish that offers like a harpooner out of Nantucket, and has never been known to break a leader. I'm just speaking about poor clowns like me."

It may be of help to those that make their own leaders to note that in tying the "blood" knot, or barrel knot, which is commonly used for this purpose, it is important to tighten the knot with considerable of a jerk rather than a slow pull. This seems to be essential to seat the coils of gut properly and make a nice, smooth knot.

There is no such thing as a perfect leader taper. But some combinations are better than others. My own preference for a ten-foot leader, tapered to 3x (the size I use the most) is as follows: .017″, .015″, .013″, .011″, .010″, .009″, .008″, .007″. Using 16 inch strands of gut, the leader length will vary according to how much is wasted in tying the knots but will be in the neighborhood of ten feet.

Another design which is good: .016″, .014″, .012″, .010″, .009″, .008″, .007″, .007″. This has the advantage of a longer point.

I prefer to taper the leader steeply at the top and more gradually near the point. This helps in casting and puts more fine gut next to the fly. Of course the longer leaders offer even more opportunity for good design.

The taper can be more gradual stepping down .001" between strands rather than .002". And one may use at least two strands of fine gut at the point, sometimes more.

I have recently been trying out some new leader designs, using nylon for the tops and silkworm gut for the points. They are tied with strands of nylon down to .011" or .010". Smaller than this, gut is used. As large diameters of gut in good grades are difficult to obtain as well as costly, this is a sensible procedure. For years I had been lead to believe that nylon and gut could not be successfully knotted together. And I failed to prove this a fallacy by not trying it. Now there is no reason not to use the two materials, as I am convinced that a blood knot or barrel knot between them, if properly tied, will never give way.

The life of any leader can be lengthened immeasurably by replacing tippets as necessary. I always carry a supply of soaked tippets, ready to add one when needed. The leader can also be made lighter and longer on the point by simply adding one or two finer tippets.

When one considers the advances in general science since our early fore-bears tried to "draw out Leviathan with a hook" and compares these advances with the slow development of angling gear, it seems remarkable that those primitive anglers were able to discover materials and adopt equipment which has actually changed very little in the ages. And, of course, it has been fortunate that efficiency in killing trout comparable with that so effective in taking the lives of humans has not been forth-coming, otherwise angling as we know it would have been relegated long ago to the pages of books.

Although rods have improved considerably over the last three hundred years, lines and leaders have actually changed very little. From the tapered, braided horsehair to the modern tapered line and leader is but a small step. Samuel Pepys in his "Diary" (1667) mentions a "Gut string varnished over which is beyond any hair for strength and smallness." This probably roughly marks the beginning of the use of some sort of gut for the "point" of the line or leader. One cannot be sure of the date silkworm gut came into use, but this "Diary" may have marked its intro-duction.

It is fortunate that the new advances in developing lines and leaders have been based on synthetics rather than on the procurement of the hair from the tail of a gray stallion or gut from the glands of a silkworm. Since the good earth, air and water supply the materials for one's new terminal tackle, one is at least assured of a good supply.

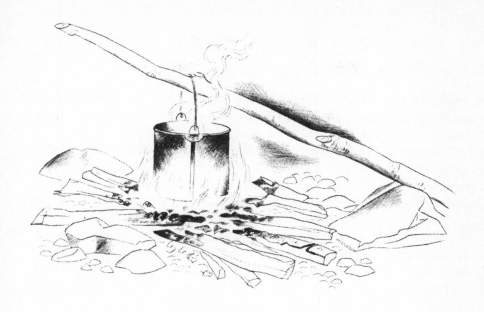

CHAPTER XIV *Ladies—and Guides*

THE READER whose wife knows what it is like to be married to a frequently absent angler and has resisted all his blandishments to convert her to an active participation in the sport should know of my own experience in this field and possibly profit by it. With the ladies, I believe it resolves to a matter, first, of comfort, and second, of catching fish.

It is quite possible, of course, that some anglers feel content that their wives do not fish. They may prefer things as they are, and look forward to their little excursions "with the boys" on which one of the attractions is a complete lack of the female. In such a case it is obvious that one should concentrate his efforts on keeping proper relationship between the home and the trout stream. He will be kept busy enough, surely, in cleaning his catch, keeping the mud of his waders from the kitchen linoleum and in general trying to placate the angling widow. Even a little gentle and judicious bribery might not be unappreciated!

After a number of excursions afield with a reluctant bride, during which her days were mostly spent shivering on the bank under a dripping raincoat and her nights tossing on a lumpy mattress in primitive accommodations, I decided I had better mend my angling ways lest I take what might become serious consequences. That was before Mr. Colt came by and did the job for me, with such good results that nowadays my arguments are directed more to restrain than to encourage my wife's ardent angling temperament.

The Colts had been going to Parmachenee in Maine for almost forty years, at least Mr. Colt, senior, had. One year, as there were no other females present, young Harris Colt's wife, Terry, needed a spot of company. My wife, Max, was invited as a non-participating angler—as a friend who might take a walk in the woods with Harris, who didn't fish much, and help to back up Terry at the dinner table when the males began to get the upper hand. At first, she wasn't interested in taking any tackle, but I surmised that once away from her family it might be possible that she would relax her antipathy toward the sport and find ways of enjoying it. At any rate, I persuaded her to include a good outfit—lending her my favorite Leonard, by the way—as I knew that poor equipment would never persuade fair lady.

The results were far beyond my hopes. First of all, it is a lovely trip in. The big launch goes up the lake for fifteen miles, then one changes to the little truck, piled high with rods and bags, for the woods road to Parmachenee, then the last lap in the boat to the island and the camp. Of course, she was made very comfortable. To be awakened in the morning by the crackle of the fire in her own cabin, and to leave a comfortable bed, really refreshed, to join friends at a bountiful breakfast certainly began the day in a manner to win admiration. When they entered the canoes, if the morning was chilly as it is apt to be in September, the guide had a big blanket warmed by the fire for her comfort. (I can imagine the sarcasm occasioned by such goings on, but I tell you it worked!)

They were frequently paddled upriver to have lunch cooked outdoors, with an occasional fish chowder, one of the notable dishes of the Maine woods. Well fortified by a brand of living in camp that she had never known, this wife of mine became interested in trying to catch some fish! The run of landlocked salmon up the Magalloway was on; she had a few lessons in casting from her guide which after my abortive attempts seemed to ring the bell, and almost before you could say "knife" she was taking fish.

Needless to say, the results of that initiation into the real pleasures of life in the woods have remained, and since then I have seen at first hand how an enthusiastic angler can be born from a great skeptic. We returned again to Parmachenee and, with the aid of experience and a heightened technique with a rod, Max turned out to be a skillful angler. Once, when a large party had gathered for lunch at the Fireplace Pool, a good salmon rose out in the pool in view of everyone there. Several tries were made by different members with various flies, without success. I finally persuaded Max to try her luck and she put on a long, fine trout leader and a small trout dry fly. With an interested but slightly skeptical gallery, including three or four guides, she lengthened her line and dropped a pretty cast about two feet above the fish. It seemed as if the whole affair had been well rehearsed. The salmon rose nobly, she hooked him fairly, and brought him into the net after the battle as nonchalantly as if she had been doing it for a lifetime. You may be sure we were all suitably impressed. The resulting congratulations were the final touch in completing her education, and from this college commencement she emerged complete with sheepskin, cap and gown.

The Fireplace was as far as we could travel by canoe up the Magalloway, and this resulted in frequent gatherings for lunch on the banks of the pool there. We could enjoy a mid-day rest and bit of good talk over our chowder or pancakes. A bit of woodsy flavor was often added by the appearance of Molly, a semi-wild deer who would come out of the spruces for her own share of our meal. She had been found an orphan when very young by a trapper who had a cabin not far from the Fireplace. He had taken her in, raised her through her first fall and winter and, the next spring, given her back to the wild. She had always remained in the vicinity, raising her yearly family and occasionally visiting her old friend for a hello and a pancake or cookie which she loved.

We first were introduced to Molly one day shortly after our fire had been started for lunch. We heard no sound of her approach, but suddenly saw her there, standing on the edge of the little clearing. Our guide, who knew her well, addressed her familiarly and tossed her a bit of lunch. Before we had left that day my wife had made such excellent friends with her that Molly ate from her hand and allowed her head to be scratched, which the guide declared was a sure sign of affection.

Each day we came there, after Molly had heard the chopping of wood and other camp sounds denoting our arrival, she would quietly appear and wait for her tid-bits. She was a greedy little beast and loved doughnuts, bacon, butter, pancakes, bananas and such a variety of stuff that we were often concerned about her digestion. The second year we were at Parmachenee, our first sight of her was at the old camp ground, the Fireplace, where she waded the tail of the big pool with a half-grown fawn. She would cautiously hide her young one in the heavy brush and then approach, as friendly as ever but often casting a quick glance backward to see to her baby. Sometimes the fawn was too curious to stay hidden, appearing out in the open to investigate. Molly would immediately return and attempt to lead it away again, not always without considerable coaxing, as the fawn seemed to want to become better acquainted The following September, the fawn appeared frequently as a yearling doe, fairly tame, but never quite so confident of our relationship as her mother who by then had taken on the fairly ripe age of nine years.

It was that same year, I believe, that we all became concerned about Molly's health. She had developed a large, hard lump on her jaw; we frequently examined it and, as we met after a day on the river, discussed her probable condition. It might have been the result of her rather outlandish diet, we surmised, but we hated to deprive her of those tid-bits which she loved so well. It has been some years now since we have been to the Fireplace and seen Molly. We have often wondered if she still may be found at our old lunching grounds, and whether she is still as fond of rich food as ever.

One September on the Magalloway gave us superb sport with the dry fly. It was astonishing how well the salmon came to the big Hewitt skater and it made for spectacular fishing. I would never have believed that fish could be coaxed up through six or eight feet of water to the surface and repeatedly at that. One evening Max took a beautiful fish of four pounds on a tiny dry fly and 3x gut, in such difficult water that angler and guide had to go ashore from the canoe and beach the fish. From then on her guide was convinced that she was the best fisherman (or woman) on the whole river!

Not many years have elapsed since that so-effective conversion. For a time it was my habit always to allow Max to precede me through the best water, and at first I was reasonably sure of finding a trout or a salmon unreached by her cast or unaffected by her presentation. It is not the same any more! Her casts cover the water to the far bank, like a true veteran; her presentation is so clever that the fish that do not rise to her fly are no more in the mood for mine, and I now find it essential to locate my own good stretches of river and cover them first if I wish to as much as even *raise* a fish.

In the summer of 1947 we were on the Deschutes River in Oregon. Conditions were not good there, and trout were very difficult. We had spent several days vainly trying to locate them or to raise them when we

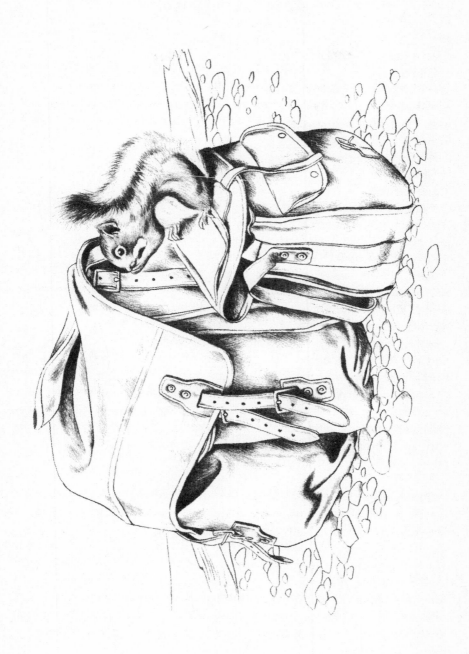

did. We had used dry flies almost exclusively and our bags had been unreasonably small.

One day I was a short distance above Max in the river, working hard over a stubborn fish which I could not get to take. Several times I noticed activity below, and finally called out to inquire what was happening. I found that Max had been very busy catching fish for some time. I called to her:

"What are you using?"

"A nymph."

"Which one?"

"The dark one, on a small hook."

It was only a moment before my stubborn trout was fastened to the end of my line, and we both enjoyed a spell of intense activity for the next couple of hours.

Her triumph was complete on that day. Since then I have asked her advice on frequent occasions which proves that her apprenticeship is ended. The pleasure of such a companionship is obvious, and for those skeptics who are still in doubt, I might add that now there is never any question as to whether or not I should go fishing. Of course, I should go, and she will go along. It has even reached a state where often I am sitting in the car, waders off, rod put away, waiting for her!

Since those days, memorable for the conversion of a non-angler into an enthusiastic one, I find at times that it requires considerable and determined effort to avoid becoming a sort of family gillie, and, like the gentleman in Henry van Dyke's admirable yarn, have thought at times of giving up angling and taking up croquet.

The conversion of the ladies to the art of angling and to life in the woods may offer problems which frequently appear at first glance to be insurmountable. Often the transition from home to camp does not bring the freedom from responsibility which usually accompanies a vacation. If the wife is cook at home, she will rarely welcome the job of doing the same thing over an open fire or a camp stove, at least, until her regard for camp life overcomes her initial dislike of the greasy skillet and a full dishpan. And cooking is hardly the only chore to be encountered. There are many tasks that may detract considerably from her enjoyment of a woods excursion.

Naturally, one thinks of a guide as a solution. A good guide is probably the best insurance for enjoyment and full relaxation that can be afforded to angler and camper. He takes over the responsibility of bed and board. Even though the wife may end by doing a large share of the work in camp, hers is still not the worry of organization. Then, too, a husband is rarely the best teacher, while the guide may give wholehearted criticism of fishing techniques, bed-making or cookery, without the usual feminine retaliation.

The following observations on guides in general may be of some interest to the reader, not only because of their relationship to the conversion process, but as a part of woods life and a member of the party. It is not only the female who needs his help, but frequently the male as well.

The American sportsman has been responsible for the building up of a class of individuals which has become quite an institution. The business man of uncertain years and increasing waistline who enters the woods is hardly able to perform the necessary jobs attending his sport. For years he has written to Harry, Pierre or Injun Joe, hoping that that worthy, with his stout back and knowledge of the country, can take on the responsibility of caring for his person, cooking his food and paddling him to where he can catch the big fish.

This dependence on a professional guide can result in two things. Admitting that either one badly needs his assistance or that one is simply averse to building a fire and cleaning fish and wants to relax instead, the guide can be a fine companion and a great help. He also can be a damned nuisance. To me, there is a combination of qualities present in the sportsman-guide relationship which makes a trip intensely enjoyable. Or the lack of them completely ruins the chances for real pleasure. In the latter case, I believe we usually have only ourselves to blame.

There are sportsmen, so called, who in their conduct toward the guide give him every reason to object or retaliate. The angler who shirks every job, complains of the food, the weather, the insects *and* the fishing may not realize how powerful the effect of such grousing may be. Be he is almost sure to be aware of the effect before his trip is over.

Most guides are men of independence. They are farmers, lumbermen, trappers and occasionally a merchant or teacher. Guiding may not be their main source of livelihood; it is usually only an adjunct to a more permanent occupation. They cannot be treated as servants, nor do they enjoy condescension and a fake affability. They are people, like the sportsmen they accompany, and only ask to be allowed to contribute their share of what can be a very satisfactory association.

Unfortunately, guides being human, with the usual human frailties, one finds occasionally an individual who mistreats one's respect and confidence. He mistakes friendliness for toadying, and respect for his ability in the woods for weakness. The result can be unbearable. The sportsman may find himself only someone who goes along with the party, doing as he is told, with no questions asked.

Of one thing I am sure. It will never pay the sportsman to be other than truthful concerning his ability with a rod or gun. Much better that he admit his lack of knowledge of the fishing in that section or his inability to track an animal properly. Better to have such things well understood in the beginning than to have to acknowledge a fault later on. An obvious desire to learn can be appreciated by the guide, even though the "tenderfoot" may be really a man of experience.

In various jaunts into new territory, or where it was otherwise necessary to employ a guide to handle the canoe or boat, I have frequently found a tendency among these men to adhere closely to the traditional in their approach to fishing. On several occasions, it was only with the greatest tact and persuasion that I obtained cooperation in trying a different or new method or an unusual place to fish. They have their favorite spots, their favorite methods and, of course, usually can put you where there are fish, the catching being up to you. If the fish happen to be taking the recommended fly or lure, all is well, but when such is not the case, the result may be a solemn declaration that the fish are not biting and it would be better to return to camp or try another place altogether.

It once took me a week to convince an otherwise excellent man that I could catch landlocked salmon on a dry fly, and *not* a Black Ghost Streamer. When he could no longer deny the efficacy of the little flies, he was as interested as a child with a new atomic water pistol and even boasted among his friends of the wonders he had uncovered. The same guide was also convinced that in certain parts of the river where we were fishing there were never any fish. No one ever caught them there so it was a waste of time trying. One day, when traveling up-river, I dropped the bow paddle long enough to make a couple of casts into one of these spots as we were passing. When a fine salmon rose and was hooked, I tactfully refrained from expressing my opinion. However, I frequently tried the same spot thereafter and many others as well, which also proved to be good fish holders.

It is difficult, at times, to convince the guide that most of the fish caught should be returned to the water. It is natural for them to like the display of a good catch brought to camp, particularly if there are other guides there, as it advertises their ability to do their job. In Maine this is seldom true as, after many years of guiding conservative sportsmen in a state that encourages conservation among the guides, they have come to the realization that more fish in the water bring more sportsmen to catch them and, consequently, greater revenue. In certain parts of Canada, where guides may be less affluent than in this country, it is customary to give them some of the fish taken, for their own use, to salt down in barrels for the winter months. There is certainly nothing wrong with this practice unless abused, as it might be when guides sell their fish to some sly sportsman who can't catch them any other way. This is hardly a frequent occurrence, however. The native guide is apt to feel that the salmon are really the property of the people who live on the river, and if he doesn't obtain them from the angler he is capable of taking them himself by netting, jigging or some other poaching method. It is better, certainly, to give away enough fish to eliminate this hazard which, if practiced enough, would seriously affect the fishing.

In a commercial fishing camp or inn, it is a different matter. There, unless caution is used, both guides and sportsmen usually have more fish than they are able to eat. The best place for those surplus fish is back in the water.

I can remember several guides who stand out in memory, not because of their knowledge of the particular water, angling technique or such, but because of some much more rare and valuable quality. One man whom my wife and I obtained to work with us had never been out with sportsmen before, but how that man could cook! He was a master of such succulences as fish chowder, one of my favorites, and he made the best pancakes I ever ate. We were the envy of our friends, even though I had to do more paddling and locate most of my fishing.

Another was a Scotsman of long years and great powers of imagination. He had the tongue—enriched with an incredible burr—to express himself and we were very apt to neglect our fishing for sheer entertainment. He had the faculty of imbuing every fish we took with a beauty and size which convinced us that we were unusually fortunate in our catches, and he always marvelled long over what was probably a rather insignificant capture.

He once related a little episode which describes him better than any words of mine might do. It seems that once each year, he and an old crony, an Irishman, also of some age, went out on a little jaunt of their own into the woods—a sort of busman's holiday.

He said, "We take a gun along too, but we don't shoot anything."

I asked him why, then, he bothered to carry it at all.

"Oh," he replied, "we just like the feel of it over our arm."

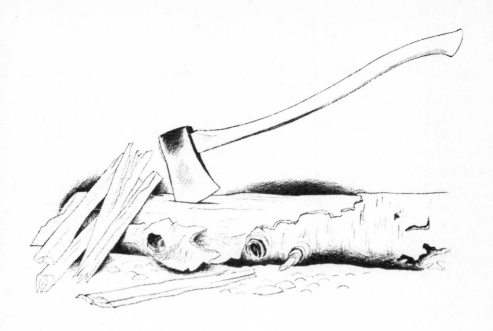

CHAPTER XV *Steelhead*

IT IS USUALLY difficult for anglers to agree on the relative gaminess of the fish they catch, each being firmly convinced that his own choice is the logical one. It has always seemed to me that the best fish is the one I am fishing for at the time. But if I could invariably have my choice of locality, river and type of fishing, I am inclined to believe that my favorite would be a fresh-run steelhead in a clear, fast stream. For sheer high-explosive on the rod they can hardly be surpassed and if one eventually beaches this streamlined dynamo, it is mainly due to the grace of the good Lord and a strong wrist.

Not that the Atlantic salmon should ever take second place to any game fish, at least for me. But the streams in which they are caught are not usually as heavy and wild as the western rivers, so naturally they do not have the benefit of the heavier current in their fighting. I am convinced that there is no actual choice between this noble fish and either the landlocked salmon or the steelhead except for the differences due to the streams in which they are taken. It will always be very difficult to make any lasting decision as to which is the best.

Probably the greatest trouncing I ever received on a stream was on a

day, many years ago, when I hooked and lost fifteen consecutive steelheads in about two hours. In all my experience, I have never had an average of losses to compare with this and yet at the same time had so much
fun and excitement. They were big fish; some of them would have
weighed twelve to fifteen pounds, and they brought to the battles a variety
and originality that were amazing. One big male, with sides red from the
fresh water, made a dash up the pool—it was a smallish stream—with
such speed that he ran cleanly out on the gravel and floundered helplessly
for a moment before he flopped his bulk back into the water. Another
leaped high against a pile of driftwood along the opposite bank and
hung himself there, half in the air until the leader broke. When the
tumult and the shouting had died away and the last fish in the pool had
been frightened into a temporary catalepsy, I collapsed on the bank, a
very tired man.

On a later occasion, in the same pool, the good Lord must have suffered a twinge of conscience, for a pair of fish was beached that day that,
by all the rules, never should have been saved at all. One of them, which
weighed 10 pounds, ran under the driftwood and hung himself up after
a highly original series of cavortings. Giving the fish up for lost, I still
wanted to save my gear, if possible, and crossed the pool at the tail,
climbing up onto the driftwood. I broke off a long, forked branch and
prodded around to clear my leader. Picture my complete astonishment
when, after a few attempts, out swam my fish, still solidly hooked! I re-
crossed the tail of the pool and beached him some distance below.

The second one, a steelhead of about 6 pounds, wrapped the leader
around a long branch which trailed in the water from a fallen tree. By
this time I had begun to be convinced that one of the more popular
subjects in the steelhead academic curriculum must have been the study of
how to throw clove hitches and bowlines while traveling at forty miles
an hour. Luckily the leader was heavier than usual and it held while I
waded across, unwrapped it and freed the fish which was by then so tired
from his struggle with the limber branch that he came in like a lamb.

I took my father along on several of these jaunts and, thank heaven,
he had a good strong heart. His first view of a hooked steelhead was when
we were fishing a pool together, one on either side. I rose and hooked a
fish which, like an angry sperm whale, rushed headlong at my father and
leaped high in the air, almost into his waders, as if it were trying to inflict
a personal injury upon him. Poor father, not being accustomed to quite
such a violent type of fishy retaliation, promptly fell flat on his back in

three feet of water. I was in a quandary for a moment as to whether I should assist one or attempt to chastise the other. But somehow I managed to see both fish and parent high and dry. The latter's only remark was that if he had known more of the belligerent propensities of that breed of fish, he at least would have armed himself with something more effective than a mere rod.

During the late summer and early fall, before the run of large steelheads began, we used to fish for what was locally called the "Blueback." These fish came up the coastal stream along with numbers of sea-run cutthroat. This was in southwestern Washington, near Gray's Harbor. No one was sufficiently knowledgeable there to determine the species of these sea-run fish, which weighed from a pound to three pounds and varied considerably as to markings. To get straightened out in our classification, which caused no end of argument, I shipped several specimens down to Dr. David Starr Jordan, the authoritative ichthyologist at Stanford University in California. He wrote me that our so-called "Bluebacks" were young steelheads, a similar fish to the half-pounders of Oregon.

The sea-run cutthroat were nearly always distinguishable by the typical red slash under the jaw which usually remained, even though most of the spots and general stream coloration disappeared in the salt water. These fish, in fine condition from the rich feeding in the ocean, gave grand sport. They were like dynamite on the rod, testing every resource of the angler. Occasionally, while fishing for this silvery depth-bomb, our fly would be taken by a heavy fish which rarely jumped but fought valiantly. These fish were young male Chinooks, corresponding to the grilse of the Atlantic salmon, and were called locally the "Jack" or "Jack salmon." Their weight was from two to five or six pounds. They were actually adults, although only of a fraction of the weight of a full grown Chinook, and would mate with the large females if the latter found a scarcity of fully grown males. Although in that particular locality I never heard of the big Chinooks being taken on the fly, these smaller fish came fairly well.

This brings up a point which also can be argued among Western anglers without any particular agreement—that of the tendency of the Chinook to rise to the fly. When I lived in the Northwest, it was not only accepted as a fact that they could not be taken in that way but no one seemed to be interested to the point of experimenting on methods which might possibly result in some discoveries. Since then, many have been caught by a variety of methods and lures unknown earlier. The locality seems to have a great deal to do with the success of the fly and, generally speaking, the streams themselves seem to determine whether success is possible. In the Southern rivers, which are frequently clear and reasonably low at the time of the salmon migrations, it is more feasible to use a fly. The fish can see it better, and are more apt to take it than when the waters are in winter spate, frequently so muddy or cloudy that fly fishing is a waste of time. Too, the better types of flies were developed only after many years of experimentation. I understand that fishing a large streamer or hair fly, which imitates the small bait fish well, is now reasonably successful in Puget Sound and around Vancouver Island, in both salt and fresh water.

I believe it will be only a question of time until methods of taking these grand game fish will be developed so that it will no longer be necessary to use the tackle which, at present, makes the sport less attractive. While on the Klamath River in northern California recently, I took my first and only Chinook on a fly and I can vouch for the fact that his gaminess left very little to be desired. Jumps are not frequent and the battle is nowhere nearly as spectacular as that of the steelhead or the Silver (Cohoe) but there are few dull moments. The exceptional strength of the fish, due to its very powerful, heavy body, is enough to test the endurance and skill of any angler, especially in the strong currents of those rivers.

Veterans of the Klamath and other streams of that section, the Eel, Smith, etc., are confident of taking the Chinook on the fly, but many had rather try for the steelheads which are almost always present at the same time. The larger Chinooks are apt to require such a great length of time to beach that frequently they are deliberately avoided, or in some cases when on the hook are even broken off intentionally. The Eel River in California, although I have never fished it and am only going on information I have received, gives probably the best opportunities for catching Chinooks. During December, January and February there are numbers of both Cohoes and Chinooks taken by fly fishing and in many cases the weights are surprisingly large.

The one salmon I took was deliberately fished for; I had seen him roll and, without changing the fly, a steelhead pattern on a No. 4 hook, I was able to hook him by getting it well down in the water. I cast upstream, and with plenty of slack allowed the weighted fly to sink. When it reached the locality of the fish I slowly worked it up and across the current and he took it after only a few tries. I understand it is very essential to use heavy flies and present them to the fish where he lies, which is almost invariably near bottom. And I am also convinced that were the

steelheads absent and the Chinook the only fish available in the river, many more Chinooks would be taken, simply because anglers would fish for them.

Just below the mouth of the Shasta River, which enters the Klamath near where Route 99 crosses that stream, is a famous riffle dubbed realistically the "Race Track." On week-ends it does resemble somewhat a sort of track meet, with many anglers jockeying for position, wading the heavy current, fishing from rocks and, very often, taking steelhead or salmon. As it is a fine salmon pool where the big fish rest before ascending either the Shasta or the main river, I made a determined effort, one day, to catch a salmon there. After fishing a fly for some time with no luck, I put on a small Indiana spinner above the fly and began to cast, allowing it to settle well down near some large rocks before retrieving it.

Very soon I had a terrific strike and the fish felt extremely strong and heavy. It did not show, but I was convinced that I had hooked a big salmon and wondered how long it would take me to kill such a fish on my light rod. I had little control over the heavy brute; the runs were very powerful and it looked as though I would be there for some time. Finally, after one wild dash the fish seemed to have got hung-up. I worked for several minutes trying to free him, but as I could feel no movement, I judged that he was gone. At last, after a great many attempts, moving position and throwing loops of slack to free the line, I felt the familiar throbbing of the fish again. I was convinced by then that the salmon would weigh 30 or 40 pounds, as I had never felt such resistance on a rod in my life.

Imagine my surprise when finally a steelhead of 5 pounds or so broke water and I could see that he was my fish. I knew at once that something unusual had happened and with my first good look at him in the water, I could see that I had him foul-hooked in the belly, near the vent. It took another five minutes or more to beach him, tail first, and still coming in much against his will. He seemed unhurt, and I released him as I felt he had well earned his freedom.

In July the first runs of steelheads appear in the Klamath, the "half pounders," which weigh up to about three pounds. As the season lengthens the fish increase in size and numbers, the very large ones usually arriving late, from October on. The most popular month there is probably October. Weather is usually pleasant then, with cold nights and warm days reminiscent of Indian summer in New England.

Although one considers the steelhead as an anadromous fish, as he truly is, there seem to be a certain number of them which become "residents," for a considerable time. They take on the coloration of the native river trout, live in places associated with fish which do not migrate and react to the fly more like an inland fish such as are found in the Pit and Feather rivers.

Algae is abundant in Klamath Lake, from which the river flows, resulting in a stream which is not clear. But at the same time, this generous supply of plant organisms makes possible immense quantities of insects and crustaceans. These, in turn, support a large fish population. I was greatly surprised at the number of medium and small sized trout there. At times they became almost a nuisance as nearly every cast with even the largest steelhead flies brought rises and strikes, some of which inevitably resulted in hooked fish.

Like many of the streams we fish at present, part of the Klamath water is controlled by a power dam. The water level varies according to power requirements but maintains a fairly regular daily schedule. Several years ago we had a camp roughly forty miles below the dam and at a location convenient because we had good water available at the best times to fish it. It was impossible to fish properly except at low water which lasted about six or seven hours each day. This meant considerable driving to reach the various riffles when they were fishable. Low water came to our camp at about 9:30 a.m., and the stream rose again about 3:30 or 4 p.m. We would drive up-river for the day's earlier fishing, when we wanted it, and down for the evening fishing. As the rise traveled down-river at about four miles an hour, we could estimate its location at any given hour with reasonable accuracy.

It was dangerous wading if one was caught by the rise of water and I saw a couple of incidents which made me wonder whether the angler involved would make shore. At places, the river would come up as much as six feet, although the average was nearer two, and there was very little warning. Occasionally an angler who was fast to a fish would forget or ignore the first signs and find himself literally swimming for his life.

Even at low water wading was not easy, the bottom being made up of smooth round stones with very little gravel. I used both felt and hob-nails, with felt as my preference although the rest of our party had better luck with hobnails. To enjoy the fishing properly, one had to develop a thorough respect for the power of the current. We used wading staffs in the bad places and they proved a boon. These useful gadgets I made myself; I would never be on difficult water without one.

Like many of our Eastern salmon rivers, the Klamath is a big stream and, as is so often the case where the fish are apt to lie along the far bank, it makes for long casts. I went prepared for that sort of thing and had some big rods, 9 to 10 feet. Along with these I took a new 8½ foot Gillum designed for dry-fly salmon and steelhead fishing. After working out the design of a modified torpedo head line for this rod, I ended by using it almost entirely. It cast nearly as long a line as the 9½ or 10 foot rods and did it very comfortably. It also handled the fish easily. After becoming accustomed to the new oufit, I doubt whether I will ever return to the heavy tackle for salmon either, unless conditions make it essential, as they sometimes do. As most of the fishing on the Klamath is with the wet fly and there is rarely need for great delicacy in presentation, I used a reasonably heavy torpedo line which aided in casting good distances.

We used nylon entirely for our wet-fly leaders and found it satisfactory. It was certainly more convenient. We tapered leaders from 15 pound test down to 6 or 4 pound on the point and had no breaks at all until weather and water became quite cold. Then even 10 pound material would test no more than 4 or 5 pounds. Early in the morning, on a few very chilly days, we noticed that the nylon broke in knotting on the fly and several fish were lost on the strike or shortly afterward. As soon as the temperatures rose we had no trouble. It is a good policy to increase the weight of the nylon in very low temperatures. The reason for the breakages we had on the Klamath still is not clear. I only know that we thoroughly tested our leaders; that they were of new material, and that they broke readily at low temperatures. It was necessary to increase the size of our leader points to 8- or 10-pound test to avoid losing fish on the strike.

Nearly all of our wet flies were tied with wings of hair instead of feathers, and were usually weighted. We used several of the patterns developed by Peter Schwab and together with some of our own inventions, they proved very successful. My own favorites, although I am not convinced the actual patterns had a great deal to do with their success, were Queen Bess and Van Luven. Also the fly originated by C. Jim Pray, called the Thor, was a fine producer. Size 4 was the most popular with us, although we used all sizes from No. 8 to 1/0. These patterns are tied commercially by Don C. Harger, 1245 N. 21st Street, Salem, Oregon, among others. He can also advise on the patterns and tackle for different localities.

It seemed to be very important to get the fly down deep and we had definitely better luck with the weighted flies. They were tied with either copper, brass or silver wire bodies. When wool or silk was used, a base of soft lead fuse wire was first wrapped over the hook. It has been my experience that a fresh-run steelhead is less selective than the Atlantic salmon, and almost any fairly gaudy fly may work. Red-and-white combinations are excellent and they seem to like orange quite well. As natural imitation seems to be unnecessary, the fly-tier may let his inventiveness have free rein. Of course favorite flies vary with the rivers one fishes, but as a rule there are certain types which are successful throughout the West, the size seeming to be more important than the pattern.

The majority of steelhead anglers fish as one would for Atlantic salmon. But I found also that a variety of methods is as effective as in any other branch of wet-fly work. One thing I believe is important—that the fly be fished slowly and, usually, the slower the better. The steelhead is more apt to take the fly when it hangs directly downstream, at the end of the cast than is *Salmo salar.* So it is good practice to fish-out one's cast more thoroughly.

I frequently cast almost directly upstream and let the fly sink very deep before beginning to take up slack. The moment when the fly left the bottom and started to swing was very apt to be best, as in trout fishing. I even took some steelheads on an absolutely dead or drifted fly, no motion whatsoever being imparted.

The waters in which steelhead lie are known as riffles, although some may be slow and fairly deep; what a Beaverkill angler would call a run would be comparable water. The fish are apt to lie anywhere from the edges of the fast water at the top of the riffle to the very tail of the flat below. Anyone knowing Atlantic salmon water would have little difficulty in finding the lies of steelhead except for a few "hot spots" that are hard to locate unless a generous and more knowing angler tells one about them.

A gaff or net rarely is seen on a steelhead river, the practice being to beach the fish instead. This makes it easy to return fish to the water, as we did in nearly every case. It is surprising how easy it is to coax a heavy fish up onto a bar without endangering the tackle. Usually, if one does it intelligently and heads the fish properly, he will swim himself right out of the water. However, one day when I was fishing for small trout with

3x gut and a small fly, a good steelhead took hold and it became quite a problem to get him out on the bank. However, I was lucky and managed it! I have tried picking them up in the hand as we do large brown trout, but I have yet to see a steelhead who didn't object strenuously to such treatment.

Luckily, the steelhead is not very timorous, for with the increase in number of anglers who fish for them it would be very discouraging if they were easily put down. They seem to rise happily when the notion strikes them, even after they have been shown an assortment of tackle which would certainly cause a brown trout to head promptly for the nearest muskrat hole. So it is possible for a succession of anglers to wade through a riffle, tossing flies about every which way, without noticeably frightening the fish. This is hardly a rule, of course, as it makes for better results in any circumstances if the fish are occasionally allowed to rest. Sometimes, after several anglers had gone through a riffle, I was able to raise a steelhead by using a very large fly, 1 or 1/0. Although we can never be sure exactly what causes the sudden change of heart on the fish's part, it may well be a slightly different presentation.

For the first time in many years we lived in tents. I had almost forgotten how much enjoyment could be had in camping out and what independence accompanies the life in camp rather than in a hotel or inn. The extra freedom more than compensated for the chores which are always a part of camp life. There were two women in our party and it was with some misgivings as to their hardihood that I approached the idea of living outdoors. My fears were unfounded as the members of the so-called weaker sex more than held their own both on the river, where they took their share of steelheads, and around the campfire, where they were usually responsible for the extra touch to the mulligan or the fish chowder. Frequently the first into the water in the morning and the last out in the evening, they were the object of more than one respectful comment by other anglers. And I can remember on several occasions when they had some handsome steelheads to their credit after the men had tried and failed.

Following is a list of steelhead flies with their dressings. This group reflects the opinions of several Western anglers who know steelhead and the best flies to take them in many localities. Don C. Harger, of Salem, Oregon, the noted Western angler and writer, is largely responsible for the collection of opinions and he tied the flies as well. They have been grouped according to their geographical importance, as each section of the West has its own favorites. No doubt any of these patterns will take steelhead in any steelhead river, but, as with flies for trout, salmon or any other game fish, each river has its special types which seem to be the most successful.

CONVENTIONAL PATTERNS

Washington patterns

Number 1   Skykomish Sunrise.
  TAIL   Red bucktail or some similar hair.
  BODY   Red chenille, ribbed with silver tinsel with a few turns under the tail as a tag.
  WING   White bucktail or polar bear.
  HACKLE   Red and yellow mixed or wound together.

Number 2   Polar Shrimp.
  TAIL   Red polar bear.
  BODY   Orange wool.
  WING   White polar bear.
  HACKLE   Deep orange.

Oregon patterns

Number 3   Umpqua.
  TAIL   White polar bear or bucktail.
  BODY   Lower one-third (next to the hook point), yellow wool; upper two-thirds, red chenille, entire body ribbed with silver tinsel.
  WING   White bucktail, with narrow strips of dyed red goose wing feather down each side. Or red bucktail down each side.
  HACKLE   Brown—put on last over wing.

Number 4   Silver Ant.
  TAIL   Yellow bucktail or polar bear.
  BODY   Silver tinsel.
  WING   Black bucktail or polar bear (no longer than hook shank).

HACKLE   Red.

(This is one of the oldest Oregon flies.)

California patterns

Number 5   Thor.
TAIL   Orange bucktail or polar bear.
BODY   Red chenille.
WING   White bucktail or polar bear.
HACKLE   Dark brown (mahogany).

(This fly was designed by C. Jim Pray of Eureka, California.)

Number 6   Golden Demon.
TAIL   Golden pheasant crest.
BODY   Gold tinsel.
WING   Bronze mallard side feathers or brown bucktail.
HACKLE   Orange.
SHOULDERS   Jungle cock.

PETER J. SCHWAB BUCKTAILS

Number 7   Queen Bess.
TAIL   Gray squirrel tail with distinct black bar.
BODY   Silver wire or silver tinsel over copper wire or fuse wire.
WING   Lower wing, yellow bucktail; top, gray squirrel tail.
HACKLE   Sometimes paired golden pheasant tippets are used as a "spike" under the throat. I prefer the fly without this spike. Otherwise there is no hackle used.

(Note: It is important that the wings of these bucktails should be tied so as to slope upward at a greater angle from the hook shank than in the usual bucktail.)

Number 8   Paint Brush.
TAIL   Red bucktail or polar bear.
BODY   Brass wire, or gold tinsel over fuse wire.
WING   Lower wing, red bucktail; middle wing, yellow bucktail; top wing, brown bucktail dyed red.

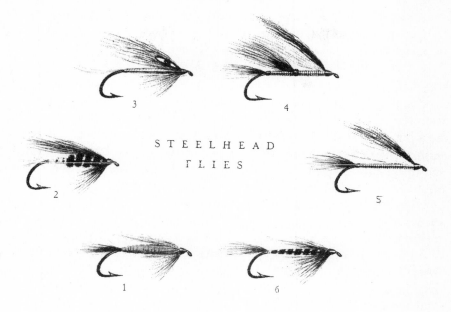

STEELHEAD
FLIES

NUMBER 1	Polar Shrimp	NUMBER 4	Paint Brush
NUMBER 2	Umpqua	NUMBER 5	Bobbie Dunn
NUMBER 3	Golden Demon	NUMBER 6	Van Luven

(See text for classification of districts)

Number 9	Bobbie Dunn.
TAIL	Red bucktail or polar bear.
BODY	Copper wire.
WING	Lower wing, white bucktail; top wing, brown bucktail dyed red.

Number 10	Van Luven.
TAIL	Red bucktail or polar bear.
BODY	Red silk floss over fuse wire or copper wire, ribbed with silver tinsel and then lacquered.
WING	White bucktail.
HACKLE	Dark brown (mahogany).

Number 11	Harger's Orange.
TAIL	Orange bucktail or polar bear.

BODY   Gold tinsel over fuse wire ribbed with fine gold oval
            tinsel or gold cord.
WING   Lower wing, brilliant orange bucktail; top wing, black
            bucktail dyed orange.

One might ask why the steelhead flies do not follow more the theory of "impressionism" than these dressings show. I can only say that this group does not contain any flies that I have designed, and my recent experience with steelhead has been too little to advise on the subject. I have depended mostly on information from Western anglers and my own small experience with some of the patterns.

I would welcome an opportunity to experiment with the "broken color" theory in steelhead flies, and believe that, as in flies for trout and salmon, the introduction of a more life-like effect would be advantageous. Certain of the dressings given contain these qualities. Tinsel is always good to augment the shimmer of the fly in the water. Some of the materials such as polar bear hair carry out well the impressionistic quality due to their sheen. And certainly "color," as such, is not lacking in the steelhead flies! They are truly colorful, sometimes gorgeous creations. It seems to me that the color could be carried further through the use of mixed colors, instead of adhering to a solid tone. Preston Jennings' "Iris" fly combines many colors. It is based on a scientific theory but the effect is truly impressionistic. It is a deadly fly.

Steelhead anglers who are fly-tiers could find a large field for experiment in the direction of impressionism, and I am sure their time would not be wasted.

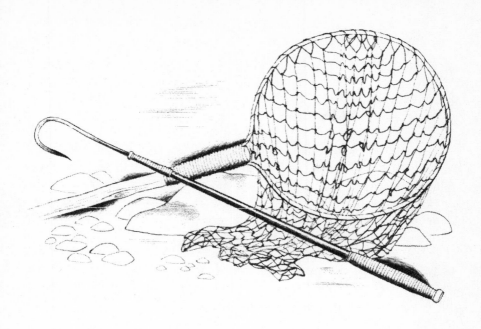

CHAPTER XVI *Atlantic Salmon*

THE GOOD LORD must have been concerned about the happiness of fly fishermen when he made the nobility and proportions of the Atlantic salmon available to them. To be sure, the Western salmon occasionally can be taken on the fly, although in most waters methods of consistent success with the big Chinooks have yet to be developed. But the Atlantic salmon is more nearly trout-like; he takes the dry fly beautifully, and is in our rivers when we are best able to enjoy angling for him. The rivers themselves are usually clear, lovely streams. Many are easily fished, with long sloping bars, clear pools where the salmon can be seen over the bottom, and the rich beauty of the Northern forests, the spruce and birches.

When the salmon comes up from his deep feeding in salt water, from the hesitant days spent lingering in the brackish mouth of his native stream, his strengthening inner urges compel the spawning migration. His big body is heavy with the fat he has stored to sustain him and the swelling milt for the perpetuation of his kind. At last he enters confidently the pools and rapids of the river. His feeding is over—or nearly so—until the return to the sea, or until his death after spawning. He is compelled by some strange urge to take occasionally the flies offered to him, and for this inexplicable compulsion all salmon fishermen thank heaven and are not too concerned about why it should be.

How fortunate that one of the largest fish caught in fresh water should be such wonderful game! It makes possible a pursuit in which a single salmon is adequate reward for a long day's fishing, particularly when the angler can see the fish he is trying to catch. Somehow the sport savors more of a complete triumph, a gratification of truly dynamic contact. We pit our skill against a worthy adversary. We are learned in our art, for it is an art to fish well for salmon; he combines his strength, cunning and knowledge of the river against us and we are fortunate to win. And our reward ends at the table with the feast which is the final test of quality for the best of game. The salmon not only feeds the angler but his guests as well.

When the trout rises to the fly we can readily understand his reasons. He is a habitual insect feeder. Not so the salmon. Are his vague memories, if one can call them memories, of early life and growth in the river responsible? We cannot say. Is it a mechanical reaction to something which appears to be alive, small enough to eat and therefore food to take? We do not know. What we do know is essential. The salmon does come to our fly and takes it, and what is responsible need not concern us too seriously.

We have, on certain occasions, seen salmon rising like trout to a hatch of fly. This is rare, but does prove that in spite of his size and the inadequate return for the effort involved, he sometimes enjoys a return to earlier feeding habits. Not that knowing this will alter too greatly our selections of flies for him; we still offer an entirely different type of lure, one based more on theory than imitation.

Salmon flies have long been in a category far removed from those used for trout, even though a few of the salmon dry flies are similar to the conventional brown trout type. Our early salmon-fishing forebears in Scotland, Ireland and England used the brilliant, colorful and sometimes gaudy concoctions developed by the professional who undoubtedly wished a higher return for his efforts, and scorned the useful but drab patterns.

These early salmon flies, and some of those still in use, suggest the unpredictable qualities of the fish itself. They do not attempt to simulate too closely the insects he fed upon in his younger days in the river but are more imaginative. With their shimmer of blended color, their glitter of tinsel and the sparkle of the plumage of rare birds, they reflect the quality of the game, his grand size and the rare sport accompanying his capture.

During the last forty years, methods of angling with the salmon rod have progressed considerably. With the advent of the dry fly, following the experiments of Edward R. Hewitt and George M. L. La Branche, the sport opened the doors to a greatly enlarged and more enjoyable field. There have been great changes in salmon tackle; the big rods, weighing several pounds, with their heavy lines and big flies are now frequently replaced with the same gear as employed in trout fishing. This has not only increased the enjoyment of using light, easily handled rods and tackle but has made salmon angling possible for those who could not afford a completely different and more expensive outfit.

The rivers in New Brunswick and Quebec where the best runs of fish occur are largely controlled by angling clubs or individuals. But there are a few streams which offer a certain amount of open fishing for the less affluent, and the entire province of Nova Scotia remains with the ownership of salmon waters in the hands of the state. It is questionable how long public fishing will be available in New Brunswick, but there still are several rivers where reasonably good fishing may be had without too great expense. The Miramichi is one, and for some years my wife and I have cast our flies upon those clear waters.

One year we found low water when we arrived there in September. The fall rains had been delayed and the heavier runs of fish had not entered the river. But these low water conditions gave us grand opportunities for the use of the dry fly. Frequently the long slow flats held numbers of fish which we saw jumping and rolling, a challenge to our ingenuity.

I believe one thing about the reactions of salmon to be reasonably certain. If you can get the fish to show interest, by various movements such as raising himself slightly from the bottom or rapidly moving his fins, he can usually be risen if the angler is patient and thorough enough. Frequently I have brought them up to a dry fly as many as six or seven times, in each case the rise seeming genuine enough but actually without the fish taking the fly.

At times salmon will rise with a variety that is certainly exciting, to put it mildly. As there is to me nothing in all angling to compare with the rise of a salmon to a dry fly, it makes the sort of sport we dream of. Once a grand fish came five times for the big Gray Wulff, each rise entirely different. He bumped the fly with his nose, very delicately. Then he pushed himself vertically half out of the water like a killer whale, the fly sliding down the side of his head. He nearly cleared the water completely, once, as if attempting to take the fly on the way down. This was a bit too much for my rather shaky reflexes, and although on most rises I could delay the strike or hold it entirely when he didn't get the fly, I took it away from him that time with a vengeance! There was one grand head and tail affair; it seemed minutes before the big tail finally disappeared. But when he really decided to take the fly, in a great swirl, turning sharply away with it, there was no doubt he wanted it, or had it when I tightened with the rod.

Once, as I walked down to a big still flat where the water was fairly deep, I began to false-cast with a dry fly, stripping off line before dropping it on the water. When about ready to cast, my eye caught the flash of a salmon turning under the surface not far from shore. I shot the line out and dropped the fly rather smartly right over him and he rose and took it as if everything had been carefully rehearsed. After a couple of jumps the hook pulled out, but it was great fun while it lasted!

There was another long, slow stretch with a big rock out in the current that broke the surface. About a half-dozen salmon and grilse were there, one day, occasionally showing themselves, and it was Max who first noticed them. I was working over some stubborn fish above, not paying too much attention to what was happening below. By the time I arrived there, after having heard several expressive sounds denoting activity on Max's part, I found her with two grilse already on the gravel, casting to a large salmon which had risen near the rock. Suddenly I saw her rod arch and then a great fish broke and fell back with a terrific splash. I began to shout advice, the guide leaped to his feet on the bank and yelled "You've hooked the big one!" and for a few minutes we were all convinced that a new family record was about to be established. Picture the ensuing disappointment and chagrin when we discovered that the fish on the line was a grilse. The big salmon had only chosen that moment to show himself as if *he* had been hooked. He was fished for later, you may be sure, but never risen.

One of the great attractions of low-water salmon fishing is that the angler can usually see the fish. In using the dry fly, most of us know that it is essential to get the fly directly over the fish for good results. In fact, I rarely fish the dry fly at all without knowing exactly where the salmon is lying, as otherwise one can waste a great deal of time and might fish all day without ever being properly over one.

On the Miramichi, one day, at a long pool with a high sand bank on the far side, we located over seventy salmon and grilse by carefully stalking them from the bank. Of course, with fish as plentiful as that, one would probably raise a fish or two at least, by covering all the water. But it is more productive as well as more fascinating to have someone watch the fish while you cast for them. The information about how they react to the fly is very useful. On that particular day, we did watch the fish. Sometimes the guide would give us instructions as to how to fish the fly and sometimes we would watch for each other.

Watching was almost as interesting as casting. One particularly stubborn but rather playful salmon rose several times to my wife's dry fly. She ignored all the others in a determined attempt to take him, which she finally did by changing her fly to a small wet. Her triumph was more complete by far than if she had simply hooked him by covering all the water. The best salmon which came to my own fly that day, after being cast over for some time, finally hung himself up on a snag and pulled the hook out.

With the water greatly below normal, that year, it took a rain to raise the river a few inches and start a run of new fish. There was a party of a half-dozen of us on a good stretch one day when the new run came through. When they announced their arrival by showing themselves at the bar below our pool, we went down to watch the migration. Wading out into the shallow water at the tail of the bar, we could see them pass by the dozens, and, if we remained motionless, they frequently would almost brush our waders in their upstream journey.

Shortly after arriving in the pool itself, they began to take well and for the next couple of hours there was a very busy and very excited group of anglers and guides. Several times there were two or three fish on at once and, with the jumping of the salmon, the yelling of anglers and the facetious advice from the bank, things were hardly dull. Frequently, a man fast to a fish at the top of the pool would come down, following the fish and displacing everyone below him; they, compelled to reel in and go ashore, usually offered generous comment on such a state of affairs. It was hardly what one associates with dry-fly salmon fishing, but produced some interesting situations!

One strong fish I hooked ran upstream and around a large rock from which I couldn't budge him. I waded out into the heavy water and by risking my neck and accepting only a modicum of the advice offered from the bank, succeeded in freeing him. Off he went at once, jumped and tore up and down the pool like mad. A few moments later he was back in the same place again, solidly anchored. By this time everyone had been literally driven from the pool in disgust by my maneuverings and I had a gallery whose remarks had changed from the general to the distinctly personal. I landed the fish just in time to escape bodily injury.

Where the Renous River joins the Miramichi near the head of tidewater, there was a grand big pool, with heavy, fast water at the head and a great deal of its length studded with large rocks. This made fine lies for salmon as they came in from salt water. High tide raised the level of the pool about a foot, up to the base of the rapids at the head, so we fished it at low water. It was wonderful to see the schools of new fish come up into the current and jump and roll with their first taste of really fresh water. Frequently we could watch them, one by one, marking a break well below, and then following the jumps as they gradually worked up into the pool and settled down near the rocks. Their lies made our fishing very much like brown trout fishing and with the increased size and power of the salmon, a great deal more exciting and spectacular.

One day I tried for a big fish that showed itself at the foot of the rapids and after a half hour got him up to the big Gray Wulff dry fly. He made a short run, with a couple of jumps, seemed to gather himself and then set off across and down the river as if pursued by all the fiends in Hades. It was the most spectacular run I had ever seen. I was too overcome by the speed and fury of it to do anything but hang on. The pool there is probably three hundred or four hundred feet wide and very long, and it was impossible to follow the fish. When he reached the end of about a hundred yards of backing, the rod dipped, there was a small snap and that was all! It was a new line too, and a double calamity in that salmon and line were both lost. I doubt very much if that startled fish ever stopped until he reached deep salt water.

Since that day I have used more backing on the reel when possible. It is surprising how fine this line can be if one uses nylon spinning line, which tests adequately for the purpose. As much as three hundred yards can be held on the average salmon reel, and Edward Hewitt uses even more. He has a very good technique for such a situation as I described. When a fish starts a long run out of the pool, it is fed line as rapidly as possible, the idea being to make a loop in the current so that the pull comes from below the fish. I have yet to see a salmon, once well hooked, lost by gaining slack, and in this case the actual slack is only momentary

until the current takes it up. Frequently the salmon, or trout for that
matter, will turn back upstream as soon as the pull from below is felt. Lee
Wulff once told me that in making his motion pictures of salmon he
loosened all pressure the moment the fish was hooked, allowing it to relax
without feeling anything other than the first prick of the hook. Then when
cameras had been set up and everything made ready, pressure was put on
the fish, who soon came to life and performed for the cameras which
could easily follow the battle.

Mr. Hewitt was on the Blackwater in Ireland, in the summer of 1947,
and told me how, on one occasion, he hooked a large fish in the tail of
a pool. The salmon took off downstream at once, steadily running line
off the reel. The gillie advised following the fish but Mr. Hewitt, knowing
his limitations on scrambling down a bank over the rocks, replied that
he was comfortable where he stood and had no intention of chasing the
fish through what, by that time, had amounted to three pools or about
eight hundred or nine hundred feet of river. The very light nylon line
stayed on top of the water and remained dry, bringing no heavy pull on
the rod such as one would feel with the fly-casting line. After a few
moments of inactivity, the salmon slowly started back upriver. When all
of the backing had been recovered and the fish worked into the original
pool, he was gaffed by a gillie who admitted afterward that he had never
seen anything like it!

Ordinarily, I had rather follow a fish if practicable, and either get
below him if he stops or keep the side pressure nearly constant, which
seems to tire them quickly. But there are occasions when other methods
must be resorted to.

When water is at average or low level, and the smaller wet flies are
employed, it is good practice to keep the line well greased. There are
several reasons for this. One is that the fly can be controlled more readily;
it can be fished as a drifted fly on a slack line and the mending process
made with less effort than if the line were wet. Another is that everything
is seen more easily. One may follow the movement of the fly, detecting an
unattractive drag, and rectify it. It is much easier to know exactly where
the fly is at any time.

When a salmon rises, the angler will know it and can act accordingly.
If the fly is deeply sunk there may be many fish that follow it and even
move to take it without the angler's being aware of what is happening.
But the rise to a wet fly on a greased line is almost as exciting as that to the
dry fly. The salmon almost invariably makes a swirl on the surface. When

the fly is missed, the angler can continue his retrieve or drift allowing more time for the fish to reconsider.

It is essential that one see the rise in order to locate the short-striking fish, unless the strike is felt. Then one may rest the fish, change his fly or do any of the things he believes will bring a return. It takes steady nerves to allow the fly to continue on its course after the huge boil from a salmon, but if one strikes at the rise without feeling the fish, he seldom will hook it.

It has been my experience that changing the fly after a missed rise makes little difference if any. And I also do not believe it essential to rest the fish after the first miss. If the salmon wanted the fly enough to come for it, he would hardly change his mind immediately. If he should miss it repeatedly, there is something wrong with the fly or its presentation. I would then rest the fish and either change the fly, preferably to a smaller one of similar color, or change position to bring the fly to him from a slightly different direction. I do not believe in flogging away at a single fish for fifteen minutes, but certainly several casts can be put over him before resting. I am speaking of the wet fly here, which is a different matter from the dry fly. It seems to me that a salmon is apt to take the wet fly more nearly at once than the dry fly. One may spend a great deal of time casting over a fish with the dry fly without putting him down.

With the wet fly, if one changes his position, that is the same as beginning over again, as response from the fish could be expected just as when he was first risen or seen. Too, a different type of presentation has the same effect; a drifted fly, for example, as against a pulled fly on a tight line. But when the salmon sees the fly come to him in a particular way, I believe he decides whether to take or not within a few casts.

The greased-line technique, with drifted fly, is an effective way of fishing, as we all know, but I ordinarily prefer the fly to have a little more cross-current movement. Naturally, the greased-line style of drift will have a little cross-current movement, as tension is gradually increased on the line. But I like it to move across even more as it goes downstream; it seems to make the fly more noticeable to the fish, or at least that has been my experience. The fly should certainly not be pulled head first downstream, in the manner I have described in the chapter on the wet fly for trout. It should drift with a slow cross-current pull, lying crosswise in the current.

There are occasions when a cross-current pull on a tight line is even better. I know salmon anglers who insist on the straight-line cast at nearly all times. This seems to me to be "too much of a muchness" for good practice, but I can vouch for their success on the average. I have noticed some of them who will cast repeatedly until the line is straight and where they want it before fishing out the cast. But how do we know that what seems a poor cast to us is not a good cast to the salmon? I would never pick up a cast once it is on the water near fish. Leave it alone and possibly the drag it takes or the strange curve that it makes downstream will be just what the fish is looking for.

One might say that until every conceivable variety of cast, drift, drag or pull has been tried out, there is no proof of which is best. All one can work from is the hypothesis that certain movements of the fly are apt to bring a better average of rises than others.

There is one noticeable fault common to many salmon anglers. They fish all parts of a run or pool with the same style of cast and retrieve. On the Miramichi there is a certain stretch of water where this method would only be partly effective. First of all, there are apt to be fish very near the bank where the angler enters the water. This water should be fished carefully and on the retrieve, the fly should be brought in very near the bank before picking up. I became aware of this situation one day, when I waded ashore after having fished from the middle of the stream. Without reeling in my line, I walked slowly to the bank and my fly swung down below me into the water near shore. The fish that took hold there nearly jerked me into the river, and it was only by luck that I held him at all. Since that time I have covered that area with care before wading through it!

The middle of the stream at that spot has some interesting possibilities. Near the center of the main current is a large rock. Between it and the far shore is a channel 40 or 50 feet in width. The rock splits the current, making a nice flow on each side of the pocket below the rock. The fish lie along the edges of the pocket, in the eddy behind the rock and in the channel between rock and shore.

Most anglers start fishing at the top of this stretch, stand in the middle of the river and cast to the far shore. They let the fly swing to cover the water near the rock and the pocket below. The salmon in the pocket are always shown a fly which is moving straight across stream on a tight line at the finish of the swing. The cast is then picked up nearly over their heads. It is only the finish of the cast that covers them.

Then, as the angler wades down through the water he comes very near to the fish in the pocket; if the angler is long-legged and has high waders, the chances are that he will be right in the pocket, and every fish there will be driven out into the channel. The invariable result is that the only salmon that rise do so well over toward the far shore. I found that by starting from far enough away, the pocket and the nearer lanes could be covered, first by a drifted fly. Then line could be lengthened and the farther areas covered in the same manner. As I waded farther into the stream I could cover the fish on the far side with a drifted fly, and those below with a cross-stream or down-and-across pull. It took a great deal longer to fish the stretch properly in this manner but the rewards were apt to be considerable.

Sometimes when a fish was raised and missed, I could bring the fly past him at a different angle or speed by altering my position backward or forward, up- or downstream. But I hardly would have been able to do so had I waded down through the one lane.

Salmon which are risen nearly downstream from the angler are often lost. This is due to the fact that the fish is apt to be hooked in the tip of the jaw. When a salmon takes the fly across the current, he nearly always turns away from the angler in rising. Then the hook is usually well fastened in the corner of the mouth. This is another reason for choosing a position, not above the fish but to one side.

"Dead" water or very slow water fishing is fascinating, but few anglers can handle such a situation properly. It is naturally a great deal more difficult to take fish there than in a rapids, or in the broken water at the head of a pool. Generally the still waters are passed by for this reason. Yet there are frequently large numbers of fish in these dead areas, resting quietly before continuing their journey upstream. I have spent a great deal of time with them, and often without any return other than the value of the experience.

During 1948, a good salmon angler was generous enough to demonstrate a type of retrieve which is often effective over such fish. First of all, he used very fine gut, and a leader 12 or 14 feet in length. The fly, a very small wet, was tied on a No. 14 double hook, for extra weight. There was very little dressing, almost nothing but a body. The line was greased, and the first casts made near the shore, as the pool was deep and fish often lay near the bank. He allowed the fly to sink for a moment, and then began a very slow retrieve. The fly was given a very tiny movement by holding the line between the second finger and thumb of the left hand while the forefinger pressed in little pulls against the line. There was no stripping in, the line was left to slowly move down with the current.

I watched the fly in the water and it had a very seductive movement.

These little jerks were given at intervals of one to three or four seconds. The fly was not picked up until it had swung almost to the bank.

Another good slow-water method consisted of stripping in line with the left hand in a slow, steady retrieve, no jerks, while the rod tip was slowly waggled up and down 3 or 4 inches. The fly had a very lifelike action in the water. This retrieve has the advantage of being useful in water with no current at all, and is not quite so deadly slow a process as the other. It is essential not to hurry any of these retrieves, but to take the whole thing very leisurely—hardly to be recommended for the high-strung individual.

Of course, a speedy retrieve is sometimes what the fish want, and the angler should always try every sort of action and speed of fly. But from my experience the slower methods are usually better in still water.

Frequently I am asked a question by some angling acquaintance that has to do with the speed of the retrieve. The question is usually put directly—"Do you believe in a slow or fast retrieve in slow water?" Such apparent simplification of angling problems always appears surprising to me. How can the experienced fisherman so neatly pigeonhole a question and expect an answer which has avoided capture for generations?

The answer is always the same—"The best retrieve is the one that hooks the fish at the time the question arises." Tomorrow may be different. All one can possibly do is to arrive at a choice by experimentation and fish the method that gives confidence, at least until he is proved to be wrong.

It is quite possible that my preference for a slow retrieve is because it suits my particular temperament; I fish it more and therefore catch more fish than by another method. The same answer holds true to a great extent with the success of a fly pattern. The angler fishes it more than any other. He uses it with confidence and therefore it works best for him.

Strangely enough, when one needs very small wet flies to raise fish in low water, the largest dry flies are often effective. And they should be bushy and "meaty" in appearance. It takes considerable good hackle to float the large hooks, so nearly all dry flies will have a bushy look whether we like it or not.

Mr. Hewitt has mentioned that he believes water temperatures have a great effect on dry-fly fishing, and my own experience bears him out. During the last season the first few days on the river brought good dry-fly fishing. At that time the water temperature was around 60°. As early frosts and cloudy, cool days brought this down to 55° and then 50°, most fish refused dry flies entirely. I could get them to come up and look the fly over occasionally, but they would rarely take. The only fish risen to dries were cast over a great many times. One grilse that I hooked must have seen the fly at least two hundred times before rising. I was interested in seeing exactly how he would react, as I knew the fish was there and it was a short, easy cast. Just as I remarked to the guide that I guessed it was no use, he rose with a rush and was solidly hooked.

One of the really good tricks with the dry fly is often ignored by anglers. This is the slowly dragging fly. After its float is completed, it is allowed to continue downstream to the end of the cast and is slowly brought around on the surface before picking up. Several times I have risen a fish while wading ashore, dragging the fly behind me. One salmon came for the fly like a torpedo, throwing spray in all directions. Luckily I had a good hold on the rod so he was hooked and landed. Sometimes the dry fly will pull under when it begins to drag across current, but even then it should be retrieved as usual, as it sometimes brings the fish up. Naturally, to pull a large fly across current and keep it on top means high grade, stiff hackle, and a light hook. I have tried the skater type of dry fly in movement but have not had sufficient opportunity to find exactly how good this method is. It should bear considerable experiment; I am convinced that methods similar to those of skater fishing for trout can be worked out successfully. The main difficulty is in the leader, which has to be fine to keep the fly well up; it is very hard to handle a salmon on 2 or 3x gut!

About the time that one believes he has learned a salmon river, the fish will put him at a loss by using different lies. The river bottom varies, of course, from year to year, due to ice or freshets, and it is sometimes difficult to discover these changes. Low-water angling is interesting for many reasons, one of which is that the angler can learn so much about the stream bottom and of where the fish lie. It is sometimes necessary to use a canoe, where wading would be the usual method of approach, just to locate fish. It is surprising how they will choose some small, insignificant-looking pocket that easily could be passed by.

One angler I have heard of uses a unique method of locating his fish. He prepares the bottom of the river in advance. During the winter months, he hauls large rocks out onto the ice at places previously chosen. He simply leaves them there until the ice melts and the rocks sink to the bottom. Later, in a pool where no fish are supposed to lie, he will walk out and take salmon to the puzzlement of all who witness.

During this last summer, a new road has been under construction along my favorite trout stream. Several large blasts were set off close enough to the river to hurl large rocks into it. Now, at low water, I can easily see how, in spite of the disturbance, I should find trout in these new spots next season. They look fishy and I am eager to try them out!

The tendency of late years in salmon fishing has run toward smaller and lighter rods and tackle. For years I hardly ever used a rod shorter than nine and one-half or ten feet, weighing from about six and one-half to seven and three-fourths ounces. The ten-foot rod, which was my favorite, was a lovely thing in the hand and threw a good line. The tip was delicate enough not to break the fine gut sometimes necessary. But I found that if I used it for dry fly for any length of time, my hand and wrist became tired and the casting suffered. Some anglers adapt themselves to the longer rods with no trouble and this has a certain advantage as there is no doubt that the extra length will generally give more distance and added control at long range. As most of my fishing has been done at shorter distances I have come to the eight-and-one-half and nine-foot rods as more suitable for me. Recently, on a Western trip where I spent several weeks on a large steelhead river, I used the eight-and-one-half-foot model almost entirely, even for wet fly.

There is no doubt that almost any rod will kill a salmon quickly enough, if properly handled. It only becomes necessary to decide which rod best suits the casting style and ability of the angler. I believe in using as light a line as possible. In low water it is less apt to disturb the fish, and floats better. The smaller rods can handle lighter lines and finer gut, although some of the big, soft rods also do this effectively.

Some anglers, including Lee Wulff, use very short rods, such as the seven or seven-and-one-half-foot models. These I believe to be too short to handle a line properly unless one is on a small stream. These little weapons will cast sufficient line for many of the small Newfoundland rivers but they hardly could cope with the distances on the large streams of New Brunswick. There is one great advantage in the short rod, however, and that is in tailing or gaffing fish when no guide is used. It is difficult to bring a large salmon in close enough to the angler with a long rod, but the little ones do the job admirably.

With the wet fly, on windy days, I still adhere to the use of the nine and one-half and ten footers with heavier lines. These rods are all made with the short detachable auxiliary butt, which is put in place after hooking a fish. It takes the strain from the wrist during the battle and keeps the reel away from the body when the rod is propped against the mid-section.

The length of time needed to kill a salmon varies considerably. Some quickly kill themselves by violent fighting and jumping. Others need forcing by the angler to prevent the battle from going on for hours. One day I witnessed a little scene on the Margaree that resulted in nearly dangerous consequences.

Lee Wulff and I had walked downriver to a good pool, named from the bridge that spanned the river at that point. There were usually a few salmon, at least, in the clear water of Ross's bridge. As we approached we saw an angler on the bank with a slight curve in his rod and his line leading out into the center of the pool.

There was no sign of movement and we judged he must be hung up. We walked up to him and asked him what was wrong.

He replied, "I've got a fish on here."

"What's the matter, is he hung up?" I asked.

"I guess not," he tendered hesitantly, "but he's been like that since nine o'clock!"

It was then bordering on lunch time and Lee and I looked at each other, trying hard to appear concerned.

"Is he a large fish?"

"Not particularly, he just won't come in, that's all."

"Haven't you tried to move him, somehow?"

"No, I'm afraid he'll get off if I do."

Lee suggested, "If you don't mind my saying so, you're apt to be here all day if you don't get that fish to move. He's simply resting on the bottom."

The man looked a bit worried but didn't reply.

"Why don't you try tapping the butt of the rod, or heaving a stone out there?" Lee said.

"Well," the man replied, "I've only caught a couple of salmon and I'd hate to lose him."

We stood and looked on for another ten minutes, during which the angler continued to stand like a statue.

We were about to leave when he turned and said, "Maybe I'd better do something, after all, but I'd certainly hate to lose this fish."

By then there were a couple of farmers standing on the bridge, offering sarcastic comments.

Lee said, "If you like, I'll toss a stone out there; that should stir him up."

The worried look of the angler deepened, but he agreed with, "Be careful where you throw it."

We each picked up a cobble about the size of a fist and Lee lobbed his out into the pool a little below the fish. It had hardly struck before there was a hysterical scream from the reel, the rod bent in a big arc and a fine, bright fish broke across the pool in a shower of spray. As the salmon fell heavily back, the rod straightened, the line fell slack sickeningly and the angler began to reel like mad. However, the worst was apparent.

One of the farmers called down, "Don't look now, mister, but I'm afraid that fish is gone!"

Lee and I looked at each other and both said the same thing— "Let's get out of here, and quick!"

Our waders may have slowed us down somewhat, but as I remember it, we ran the next couple of hundred yards in a dead heat, and the time must have been close to a record.

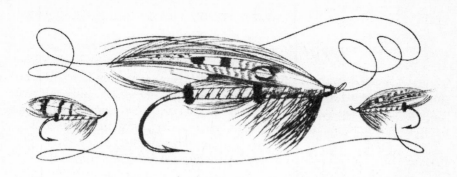

CHAPTER XVII *Salmon Flies*

As OUR entire approach to the salmon fly is dictated by the willingness of the fish to take it rather than by its resemblance to anything in nature, we use a different basis for our theorizing than in trout fishing. This allows for considerably more variation in form and color, particularly the latter, and above all in size. Salmon flies are made in sizes from the tiniest of creations on No. 12 or even No. 14 hooks to the great "6-inch irons" of the large waters and early-season fishing. The fish vary, not only in size and disposition, but according to the season. For this reason the flies used are great in number and variety.

In tying my salmon flies I still believe in adhering to certain qualities common to all underwater and overwater insect life, although the impressionistic theory of trout flies is hardly applicable in the same way. There can be impressionism in all flies to a certain extent. The effect of broken color, the shimmer of good materials is typical of many standard salmon wet flies.

Whenever one simplifies his flies so much as to eliminate many of the fancy colored feathers or other materials, it is good practice to make those few remaining materials good ones. One should not lose the qualities of color and form inherent in good impressionism but should retain that broken-color look as much as possible. There are some successful patterns which ignore these theories, as there are exceptions to most rules, but I believe that anglers could improve even these exceptions by experimenting with different materials which would add to the effect of life likeness and still not alter the basic design.

Each year that I fish for salmon I find the smaller, more lightly dressed

167

wet fles are becoming my choice over the larger patterns of conventional construction. All salmon anglers probably have noted how patterns are becoming more like trout flies in their color and design than was the style in the past. As angling traffic on the rivers increases and the fish become fewer and warier, it may become necessary to adopt methods more like those used for brown trout than for salmon.

Particularly on the Miramichi, where most of my fishing is done, conditions are apt to make the orthodox methods unproductive. On my last trip there the water was extremely low, and I had to use smaller flies, finer gut and more experimental methods than ever before to raise the fish.

Most of the salmon were hooked on No. 10 wet flies, and I used No. 12's and even 14's at times. The fish seemed extremely shy and were apt to come short, a great deal. Frequently I would have three or four rises to the same drift or retrieve without contact at all. Large, bushy flies were of no use whatever, and the only flies larger than No. 8 which caught fish had been reduced to a mere body, with no wing and little hackle, if any.

In tying these low-water flies, I found it important to make them thin and streamlined. A small, tapered head was a help, as it made a better entry into the water, and the fly did not tend to swim up on the surface leaving the wake which is such a nuisance. The angler should always try his fly, when first tied on, in the water close by, to see how it swims. One is apt to fish a fly for some time without realizing that it is swimming sidewise or upside down. This often occurs when the leader point is fairly heavy as the gut often will not allow the fly to take its natural position unless it is tied on with care.

When fishing very slow or dead water, the importance of the fly's riding position cannot be overrated, as in water of that type each defect of presentation is so easily detected by the salmon. A fly is apt to ride up on the surface in still water. The leader may tend to float and such a combination is not good.

The type of hook used has considerable bearing on the way the fly will swim. Ira Gruber, a salmon angler of many years' experience and an excellent fly-tier, uses only the offset Model Perfect for his salmon flies. One of the reasons for his choice is that he believes many other hooks cause a wake under water which takes the form of a stream of air bubbles, and makes the fly appear much larger than it actually is.

I have seen effects of this sort myself, but had not felt that it was a serious problem. But as Mr. Gruber is an enthusiastic student of angling

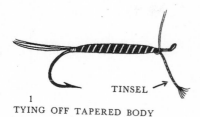

1
TYING OFF TAPERED BODY

2
CUTTING OUT
SECTION OF HACKLE

3
TYING IN HACKLE

4
UNDER WING TIED IN

*Showing method
of tying "down-wing"*

and an observant man on the stream, he may have an argument which will bear investigation.

Mr. Gruber's flies are models of perfection. He has a method of winging that produces one of the best types of "down-wing" I ever saw. Charles De Feo is another tier who seems able to conquer this aggravating problem, one which probably will badger me for the rest of my days.

The most effective low-water flies are invariably streamlined. The wings should be low over the back, not so upward-sloping or upright as in most trout flies. And the tent-wing type is particularly effective when feathers such as mallard or wood duck are used. These rather obstreperous feathers are difficult enough to handle conventionally, but when one attempts to build a good tent-wing which lies well down over the back of the fly, he is in for trouble.

There are several things one may do which will help in achieving a good winging job. One is to properly taper the body toward the eye of the hook so that the wing will not be forced upward by the bulk beneath it. Another is to use hackle sparingly, and not wrap a bushy mass around the shank.

Charles De Feo showed me a very interesting and effective method of tying a down-winged fly, and I will try to explain it here. First, build your body, smoothly tapered at both

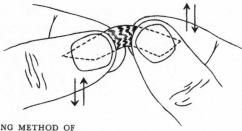

5
SHOWING METHOD OF
"HUMPING" WING FEATHER

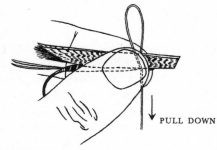

PULL DOWN

6
SHOWING USE OF LOOP
IN TYING IN WING

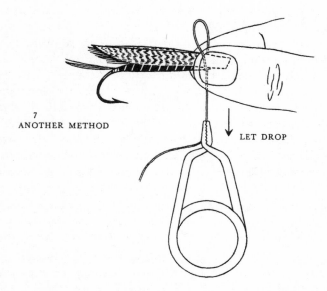

7
ANOTHER METHOD

LET DROP

Showing method of tying "down-wing"

ends, leaving sufficient bare hook shank near the eye for hackle and wing. Body material, ribbing, etc., should always be tied in *under* the hook shank to eliminate lumps on the top of the body where the wings will go. In fact this procedure should always be followed in either tying in or tying off any materials in salmon fly construction, with the exception of the wing itself. (See illustrations, Figure 1.)

To hackle the fly, take a hackle feather with barbules of the proper length and snip out a small section of the center rib as shown in Figure 2.

Holding this segment of the hackle by the barbules and *underneath* the hook, tie it in with two or three turns of silk as shown in Figure 3. The center rib of the hackle should not project back of the point at which it is tied in. Only the barbules will show. Clip off the exposed rib and barbules at the head of the fly. This method of hackling is an excellent way to avoid bulk. As most wet flies are much too heavily hackled anyway, the few sloping barbs are all that are needed to give life to the fly and retain its streamlined form. Now there is no hackle over the back of the body which will interfere with tying in the wing, nor do the hackle ribs, which ordinarily occur in a bunch at that point, cause a clumsy bump on the body.

Many of the down-wing type flies are made with an under wing, such as in the "Oriole" pattern. This gives substance to the wing and, with its suggestion of half-hidden color seen through the thin mallard feathers, adds to the "shimmer" of the fly and makes it truly impressionistic. The golden pheasant breast feather used for the under wing on the "Oriole" can be tied in in a number of ways. Usually, I simply pull off a segment from each side of the feather, match them and tie in with, at best, two turns of silk. One may use hackle barbules or even hair for this under wing, bunching it together and tying in directly on top of the hook. The under wing should project slightly beyond or in back of the over wing. (Figure 4.)

The mallard feathers for the over wing are then chosen, a matched pair, and a section of each cut out from opposing sides of the feathers so as to form the matching curve when placed together. Before tying these in, it is good practice to work them over a bit between the thumbs and forefingers to help curve the sections properly and even up the tip ends. A sort of seesawing motion is used, holding the sections firmly to prevent separation of the fibres and gradually working them into the shape and curve desired. (Figure 5.)

Take these feathers in the left hand between thumb and forefinger and place them on the hook so that the butt of each comes down slightly over the side of the hook shank. They should not be tied directly on top of the hook. Then pass the tying silk over the butts in a loop, bringing this loop between the fingers of the left hand before tightening the thread. Squeeze it tightly with the fingers that hold the feathers, and pull *down* on the silk to tighten it. Repeat this two or three times before releasing pressure with the left hand. (Figure 6.)

The wings may also be tied in one at a time, preferably the one on the far side of the hook first.

Another way of tying is as follows: Fasten a pair of heavy hackle pliers to your tying silk (unless you use a bobbin, which will work if it is heavy enough). Make the loop over the butts of the wings and hold it squeezed between the fingers of the left hand as before. Then grasp the butts of the wings with the right thumb and forefinger, simply letting go of the loop of silk in the left hand and allowing it to drop. The bobbin will pull down on the wing and hold it in place. Repeat this two or three times. (Figure 7.) Keep the head of the fly small and tapered to insure good entry.

It seems that no matter how many flies the angler takes with him on his trips there are usually one or two "killers" that he finds lacking. Conditions change with the years, and the fly or the technique that is effective one season may be no good the next. The angler may develop a killing fly on the spot, once he knows conditions first-hand. I always carry with me some sort of fly-tying outfit, even though it may be a rather abbreviated one. Almost invariably I will be able to improve my fishing either by working out new patterns or altering old ones. It is surprising how small changes in size or in the amount of dressing will sometimes bring success when one is having trouble in raising or hooking fish. During 1948 the best flies were extremely thin and lightly dressed. On several occasions I was able to bring up the fish only by removing literally all of the dressing from the fly except the body, and picking out the dubbing a bit to give it a little "movement" or "character."

If the angler spends his evenings tying flies in some out of the way camp, he is apt to be at a loss for proper light to work by. I can remember only too well the trouble occasioned by trying to work properly with inadequate light. In recent years I have included in my kit a good, strong, adjustable electric lamp of the reflector type. I have blessed the convenience it brings many times, and will continue to take it along, although when I pack the car it seems a nuisance. Where there is no electric power available, some sort of powerful gasoline lantern is the next best bet.

One of the best portable fly-tying kits I ever saw was made from a mechanic's metal tool box equipped with a series of trays which were hinged so that they pulled to the sides when the box was opened, allowing the entire contents to be seen at a glance. It was practically indestructible and easily held a great deal of material.

Charles Phair once told me, before he was called to the happy fishing grounds, of some methods he employed in angling for stubborn fish. He said that he always carried a few variations of a fly called the "Fat Mary." This was no standard pattern nor did it adhere to a single type of dressing. He made it as a "last resort" fly, one to use as a finishing off, in late evening or over a fish which he had been unable to move. He tied it on large hooks. First of all, it was made with a very fat, heavy silver body. Then, all of the brightest materials he could find were tied on for wings and hackle—Indian crow, chatterer, toucan, the gaudiest dyed feathers and hackles. Even tinsel was used for hackle at times. This striking creation was shown the salmon and many were the tales of how well it worked.

In my own experience, I have found that this idea should not be ignored. One of the best fish I ever took, not only for size but for the most violent fighting qualities, rose to an enormous "Torrish," a fly which could hardly be anything but the result of pure imagination in design. I had worked over the fish for a long time, but the first cast with the big, golden creation brought him up with a rush which very nearly jerked the rod from my hand.

On his first wild dash for freedom, he circled a big rock below me and while my line still pointed downstream he leaped high in the air at least a hundred feet upstream. For a moment I thought it was another fish, but soon became aware of my predicament. I finally freed the line and took up the big-bellied slack, finding the fish still on. He repeated this performance again later on, then rushed down through a long heavy rapid while I stumbled along behind, hoping for the best. It was a good half hour from the time he was hooked until he was on the gravel. He had a long, livid scar across his side with an open wound at the bottom. Some predator, or some poacher with a spear had almost ended his life, but certainly not his spirit.

Here is the list of my favorite wet flies and their dressings for those who might be interested in trying them out. I have tried to reduce the long lists of patterns to a few—light, medium and dark. If the angler can be equipped with these in small, medium and large sizes, he is pretty apt to handle most situations. The Jock Scott dressing has been reduced to bare essentials, as have some of the others, but the results are as good when fished, and of course that is what counts. The hook sizes for the different patterns below are for the conventional irons. If the low-water type of hook is used they should run from about No. 10 to No. 2, with the dressings proportionately smaller.

Beginning with the light flies the dressings follow:

Number 1	Silver Gray.
TAG	Silver tinsel and yellow floss silk.
TAIL	A topping (from the crest of the golden pheasant cock).
BUTT	Black ostrich herl or black wool.
BODY	Wide, flat silver tinsel, ribbed with oval silver tinsel.
HACKLE	Badger (Throat only).
WING	If feathers are used, widgeon side feathers, a topping over. If desired, a touch of color may be added by introducing married strips of yellow, white and green swan. To wing a fly in this manner I first tie in the strips of married feathers, and then over them, but not covering them completely, the widgeon or whatever other feathers are used. It is sometimes difficult to obtain widgeon, teal, mallard or pintail feathers large enough for hooks of size 2 or 1. I frequently use Egyptian goose for winging in that case. These barred feathers make excellent wings for any fairly light fly. If hair is used for the wing, gray squirrel tail is good, with a topping over. When hair is employed, I sometimes introduce a few strands dyed red, yellow, blue or green or a mixture of some of these to give an added touch of color and shimmer.
HOOK SIZES	10, 8, 6, 4, 2.
Number 2	Blackville.
TAG	Silver thread and orange floss.
TAIL	A topping.
BUTT	Black herl or wool.
BODY	Embossed silver tinsel.
HACKLE	Bright orange (Throat only).
WING	Widgeon or pintail, a topping over.
HOOK SIZES	10, 8, 6, 4.

Number 3   Cosseboom.
TAIL   Bright green rayon floss.
BODY   The same green floss, ribbed with wide, flat silver
              tinsel.
HACKLE   Yellow, rather long.
WING   Gray squirrel tail.
Cosseboom always tied his hackle on last, after the wing, so that the
wing lay nearly flat along the back of the hook shank with the yellow
hackle over it.
HOOK SIZES   8, 6, 4, 2.

Number 4   Oriole.
TAIL   A few brown hackle barbules.
BODY   Black seal's fur or wool ribbed with very narrow oval
              silver tinsel. The body should be tied rather fat and
              heavy.
HACKLE   Red brown, rather sparse.
WING   An under wing of the red breast feathers of the golden
              pheasant, and over this, but not entirely concealing it,
              the outer wing of dyed yellow mallard side feathers, tied
              tent shape and well down over the body.
HOOK SIZES   10, 8, 6.

Number 5   Half-stone (my own adaptation).
TAG   Silver tinsel.
TAIL   A topping—or a few strands of some speckled feather
              such as wood duck.
BODY   First third (nearest the curve of the hook)—yellow
              seal's fur; second two-thirds—black seal's fur. Ribbed
              with narrow oval gold tinsel.
HACKLE   Black or dark furnace.
WING   Quite thin and short, of the speckled hairs at the base
              of the fox squirrel tail.
HOOK SIZES   10, 8, 6, 4.

Number 6   Abe Munn "Upriver."
TAG   Silver tinsel.
TAIL   Either a few brown hackle barbules or a few strands of
              bronze mallard or turkey.

BODY	Cream-yellow seal's fur. (This body can vary from pale buff to bright yellow.) Ribbed with narrow oval gold tinsel.
HACKLE	Red-brown.
WING	Turkey, bronze mallard or brown speckled hen. Should be mottled brown color, whatever is used.
HOOK SIZES	10, 8, 6.

Number 7		Jock Scott
	TAG	Silver tinsel.
	TAIL	A topping.
	BUTT	Black herl or wool.
	BODY	In two equal sections—first (nearest the hook point) of yellow silk floss, second of black silk floss, both ribbed with oval silver tinsel.
	HACKLE	Black, and if you wish, add a few turns of guinea hen to the black. (I use hackle only on the throat of the fly.)

Legend for color plate on inside back cover

SALMON WET FLIES

NUMBER 1	Silver Gray	NUMBER 6	Abe Munn "Upriver"
NUMBER 2	Blackville	NUMBER 7	Jock Scott
NUMBER 3	Cosseboom	NUMBER 8	Bastard Dose
NUMBER 4	Oriole	NUMBER 9	Squirrel Tail
NUMBER 5	Half-Stone	NUMBER 10	Mink Tail,
	(on low-water hook)		(on low-water hook)

SALMON DRY FLIES

NUMBER 1	White Wulff	NUMBER 4	Macintosh
NUMBER 2	Gray Wulff	NUMBER 5	Pink Lady Bivisible
NUMBER 3	Hunt's Teagle Bee	NUMBER 6	Stone Fly

STEELHEAD FLIES (wet) (pages 147–150)

NUMBER 1	Skykomish Sunrise	NUMBER 4	Queen Bess
NUMBER 2	Silver Ant	NUMBER 5	Harger's Orange
NUMBER 3	Thor		

(See text for classification of districts)

WING	Bronze mallard side feathers, a topping over. Color may be added as suggested with the other patterns in red, yellow and blue.
HOOK SIZES	8, 6, 4, 2.

Number 8   Bastard Dose.

TAG	Silver tinsel and yellow-orange floss.
TAIL	A topping.
BUTT	Black wool or herl.
BODY	A short section, first, of light blue seal's fur or wool, the rest black seal's fur; both ribbed with oval silver tinsel.
HACKLE	Claret (throat only).
WING	First, an under wing of a pair of golden pheasant tippets, back to back, over which is tied a wing of dark teal. In the larger sizes, I usually cover the top or back of the wing with strips of bronze mallard, a topping over all.
HOOK SIZES	8, 6, 4, 2.

Number 9   Squirrel Tail.

TAG	Silver tinsel.
TAIL	A topping or a few brown hackle barbules.
BODY	Black wool or seal's fur ribbed with narrow oval silver tinsel.
HACKLE	Red-brown.
WING	Fox squirrel tail, with a black bar and orange-colored tips. The wing I like best on this fly is made from the hair of the Canadian pine squirrel, but as this tail is sometimes difficult to procure the fox squirrel is next best.
HOOK SIZES	12, 10, 8, 6.

Number 10   Mink Tail.

TAG	Silver tinsel.
TAIL	A topping or a few hairs from the mink tail.
BODY	Black wool or seal's fur, ribbed with narrow oval silver tinsel.
HACKLE	Black.
WING	Mink tail hair—not too heavy.
HOOK SIZES	12, 10, 8, 6.

The angler who ties his flies may work out his own versions of many salmon patterns by reducing the quantity and variety of material and substituting hair for feathers when desired or practicable. It has always seemed to me that most of the complicated flies were designed more for the show case than for the water, and the result is that heavy prices have to be charged for such exacting work. I have never found it necessary to use flies of this sort to take fish, and if the angler's fly-tying skill or resources are limited, he should experiment on the various simplifications. We do know that certain patterns, such as the Jock Scott and others, have always been very successful as originally dressed. We can adhere to these old stand-bys to a certain extent by trying to retain the general effect of the fly in the water. The body, I believe, is most important, and it is easy to retain this while achieving economies in the wings.

The hook sizes given here are reasonably small and it is in these sizes that the simplified patterns are the more practical. My own experience has been mostly with small and medium-sized flies; the larger ones occasionally used were nearer to the standard dressings. I can hardly advise on how successful the simplified type would be in those sizes. But I see no reason to doubt their effectiveness.

The hair flies used in the type of slack-line fishing known as "fishing the patent" have not been mentioned, as I have not had sufficient experience in this style of angling to speak of it authoritatively.

To the list of wet-fly dressings I will add my favorites for dry flies as well. The same suggestions both with dry flies and with wets hold true as to changes and additions by the tier. As nearly all of my best dry flies are of a medium color shade, with the exception of the White Wulff and one black-bodied fly, there is little reason to list them from light to dark.

The hooks used are necessarily lighter in weight and I prefer a bend on the order of the sproat. The Hardy dry-fly hook is excellent, but has been hard to obtain in recent years. The Model Perfect is good, of course, except that these hooks in large sizes with light wire construction have been rare as well.

One thing about dry-fly hooks is important. The loop eye is better than the conventional eye. It eliminates the danger of gut breakage caused by roughness on the end of the wire. In using the conventional eye, whether plain or tapered, I always wrap my tying silk around the shank next the eye to obviate this trouble.

Number 1   White Wulff.

TAIL   White bucktail or some other white hair, fairly stiff and crinkly.

BODY   Cream-colored fur or wool, tied rough and rather heavy.

WINGS   White bucktail or same as tail.

HACKLE   Badger. On the larger sizes I use three and sometimes four hackles, tying them in with the good side facing the curve of the hook. The last hackle nearest the eye can be tied in as usual.

HOOK SIZES   10, 8, 6, 4.

Number 2   Gray Wulff.

TAIL   Brown bucktail or Chinese deer tail or fox squirrel tail.

BODY   Muskrat fur or a mixture of dubbing to make a gray of medium shade, tied rough and heavy.

WINGS   Same as tail.

HACKLE   Medium dun.

HOOK SIZES   10, 8, 6, 4.

Number 3   Hunt's Teagle Bee.

TAIL   Dyed red bucktail or some fairly stiff hair, not too long.

BODY   Alternate bands of yellow and black wool, about two bands of each color.

WINGS   None.

HACKLE   This can be a mixture of brown, black and grizzly; or as I sometimes tie it, brown and grizzly mixed. Or ginger can be used instead of brown.

HOOK SIZES   8, 6, 4.

Number 4   Macintosh.

This fly can be tied in any number of variations. The original Macintosh dressing is given below, but I also use hair of several different colors for the tail as well as different combinations of hackle. For instance, I like fox squirrel for tail and a mixture of brown and grizzly for hackle. Or gray squirrel for tail and the same color for hackle. The following dressing is from a fly tied by Dr. Edwards Park.

TAIL   Fox squirrel, rather bushy, and tied in at the base of the hackle, or at about the center of the hook shank.

BODY   None.

WINGS   None.
HACKLE   Dark ginger or light red-brown.
HOOK SIZES   10, 8, 6, 4.

Number 5   Pink Lady.

Bivisibles of various colors. These can be made in a variety of sizes and colors from light ginger to very dark brown or gray, and on hooks from No. 10 or 12 up to No. 4. The largest variation, however, is not so much in hook size but in diameter of hackle. The largest flies should be one and one-half inches or two inches in diameter and very bushy. Combinations of colors are good, such as the old reliable grizzly and brown, and Mr. La Branche's Pink Lady bivisible is excellent. The dressing for this fly is given below.

TAIL   Dark ginger hackle barbules.
BODY   Pink silk floss, ribbed with flat gold tinsel.
HACKLE   Body hackle of dark ginger tied palmer fashion over the silk and tinsel. Then a pair of hackles of the same dark ginger tied in near the head. Finally a single hackle of pale yellow at the head.
HOOK SIZES   10, 8, 6, 4.

Number 6   Stone Fly.

This dressing was given to me by Frederick Hollender. Whether he is the originator of the pattern I am not sure. It is an excellent killer and is very good tied on the larger hooks.

TAIL   Black hair. I like calf tail best for this as it is a crinkly hair. The tail should not be too long, and I sometimes tie this fly with no tail at all.
BODY   Black seal's fur. This can be a mixture of dark fur such as mole with some other fur to give it a mixed look (over kapok in the larger sizes to aid in floating the fly). The kapok is spun on the tying silk and wound on similarly to any dubbing, rather heavily. Then the body material is wound on to cover it.
Wings   Fox squirrel tail, tied rather bushy, and nearly flat over the back.
HACKLE   Brown, tied on after the wing, and wrapped over the butt of the wing, next the eye of the hook. I use four hackles on this fly in the large sizes.
HOOK SIZES   8, 6, 4, 2.

CHAPTER XVIII *The Neversink*

ONE OF the most pleasant assocations of my fishing career was with
Edward Hewitt on his Neversink water. The many days spent at the old
camp with the rearing pools down in front, the long roof of the hatchery
under the slope at the side and, across the meadow, the Camp Pool showing dark against the hemlocks, have brought with them an apprecation
of how complete can be the angler's reward, not in mere numbers of trout,
but in a renewed appreciation of those completely satisfying moments
which every true angler experiences from time to time.

Perhaps it would be a trip to the Big Bend in that incredible old Buick
with the holes in the top for the rods, and the rough woods road that
would be taken so vigorously by Mr. Hewitt, a driver whose speed and
dexterity hardly comported with his advancing years. The wonderful pool
itself, with the current running deep along the vertical rock, and the clear
water like a reading glass over the sand at the tail. There you could see
the trout so well that it was a great treat as well as great sport to bring
one up from the bottom to your fly.

There were many lunches on the high bank above Mollie's Pool, where
we could watch a big trout feeding below in a pocket near the bank
while we broiled a small one on a stick. There was a real whopper under
that old fallen tree and we planned our strategy to outwit him.

The Little Bend was a great attraction as well. We would drive up to
York's Ford, wade the river and follow an old path along the far bank

through the rhododendrons. In late June and early July, it was like walking through a great conservatory a half mile long. The heavy clusters of blossoms brushed us as we passed and left their petals like snowflakes on our shoulders. At the bend, the river pushed its current against a long submerged ledge which overhung deep water and hid the big trout in its shadow. But they moved out at times, and when we saw the little dimples drop down with the current, we would try not to be too clumsy in our casting. The trout in that pool were wary; I imagine that the ones which finally came to our flies were the less experienced, and I always wondered, when we unhooked them and sent them back with our blessing, whether they communicated their adventures to their brethren.

Mr. Hewitt had greatly improved his water and his fishing by building a series of dams, and when he put in a new one which made the Shop Pool, a large rock at the head became a favorite hide for good fish. It was difficult to resist a few casts in passing and I rarely went by without a try or two. There was always a trout there, so the spot was always fished with enthusiasm. If we caught its tenant, it was only a short time before another would be using the same lie. The fly had to pass the rock within an inch or two, and the best place was where the water curled around it. The fly appeared particularly attractive as it rode the little crest and slipped past. A heavy swirl below the rock meant that the trout had been late in his decision and after overtaking the fly had turned to seize it.

Some of the finest water was in the Camp Pool. There the river ran along a vertical rock wall for a hundred yards before it slowed and flattened to a wonderful big tail. The trout loved the very edge of the rock, and the overhanging trees made it a grand place to show our skill, or lack of it. Once, there, I had been given a chance at a fine heavy fish that Mr. Hewitt had located. After considerable casting and several fly changes, and of course when I was least expecting it, the fish rose beautifully—and I left the fly in his mouth. My resulting confusion gave the old master at my elbow reason for a chuckle or two, but he was generous and didn't laugh too long!

He and I used to fish the big Flat Pool together. It was nearly eight hundred feet long, thigh deep except near the bank where it was deeper and wide enough for two rods. The fish were distributed along the banks of the pool, so we would take a bank each and work up the pool side by side. It was the perfect combination of angling and companionship as we cast steadily and passed our comments back and forth. The branches overhung the water as much as fifteen feet, sometimes nearly touching it. It was great fun to get the fly well back in a difficult place and see the boil that indicated a good fish. The big spiders worked well for this, and I was shown how to cast them to bring out the trout that were difficult to approach.

Mr. Hewitt has made a great many contributions to angling, one of the most noteworthy being a willingness to try unorthodox methods. The invention and use of the big spider, the "Neversink Skater," is a good example. It was invaluable for fishing under the bushes where the line had to be driven in with considerable force. The greater air resistance of this fly always caused it to come down gently.

He tied his skaters on a light No. 16 hook and the diameter of the hackle was from 2 to 2½ inches. No body or tail was used. It was simply a pair of hackles wrapped around the hook shank. The favorite color on the Neversink was red-brown, and the hackles were as stiff as could be found. He kept the fly moving in quick jerks, bounces and draws which proved very deadly to large trout.

The big trout under the fallen tree at Mollie's Pool was in a tiny eddy beyond a swift current. It was very difficult to get a fly to him at all. The big spiders came in handy here. When the cast was thrown, the spider was immediately made to jump across the eddy, the line being held clear of the current as much as possible. The unavoidable "drag" was thus converted into a distinctly attractive movement which enabled me to hook that "Aunt Sally" solidly on several occasions, only to lose him in the dead tree each time.

Probably the best place of all for the skater was under the dams. These low dams made fine holding pools out of otherwise unproductive riffles and flats. They were built two logs high, and faced on the upstream side with heavy planks running from the top of the dam to the stream bed at a long angle. The falling water dug holes back under these dams, making fine hides, and there were always big trout in them for us to try to lure out.

As the sun left the water in the evening, the fish would move out gradually and begin to feed. We would cast the big spider up close to the foam and broken water, even into it, and work it back in jerks. Frequently a fish would leap fully out and take the fly in his descent, a thrilling sight and one of the reasons the big spiders make such exciting fishing. Sometimes a fish could be teased into a rise, with many casts. Or one might approach the fly repeatedly, even rise and miss it; but usually if the trout was not pricked he was not put down.

This fishing took nice judgment and manipulation. If the fly was moved too fast, the fish was apt to miss it or be lightly hooked; if too slowly, he might not become excited enough to go for it. Sometimes bouncing or bumping the fly had a deadly appeal. A breeze helped, as well as a downstream or quartering cast. With a fairly long rod, and a light line which aided in keeping line and leader free of the water, only the fly touched lightly in little hops here and there. Needless to say, this could hardly have been done on a long line.

During the summer evenings the fish almost invariably rose in the big flats just before dark. Mr. Hewitt had developed a surprisingly effective method for this difficult risers, using a small, very thin and streamlined wet fly with the hackle clipped off top and bottom and a thin, sloping wing. Even this dressing was sometimes reduced in size if the fish came hesitantly. As the trout were usually cruising, it required nice judgment to place the fly where they could see it. It was almost like leading a bird by swinging the gun ahead of him.

It was really a joy to cast with the tackle used for that fishing. Mr. Hewitt spliced a long leader of about 14 feet to a light line which was handled by an eight-foot rod of quite soft and slow action. He used a deliberate swinging cast, similar to that with a two-handed salmon rod, and it made for particularly delicate fishing. I grew to love that last hour on the flats those long evenings, and ten o'clock suppers were our rule.

Occasionally very small dry flies, about No. 20, were used during those late hatches but as I remember it the wet fly seemed to produce the best results. In fishing the flats during the day, when trout came poorly to the dry fly, Mr. Hewitt usually employed a wet fly like the one described and fished it close to the banks, underneath the branches. He cast nearly straight across stream, or at a slight angle up or down, and the fly had to be presented within a few inches of the bank in most cases to raise the fish. He usually added a very slight motion to the rod in retrieving.

It was on this lovely clear river that I got my fill of catching big fish and realized how disappointing it can be. My largest brown trout was taken in the Shop Pool at high noon on a bright day. He came to a small variant, out in the open water, and for some moments I was under the impression that it was only a medium-sized fish. Then suddenly he was very heavy on the light gear and made two or three fairly good runs. The rest of the battle was a grim tug-of-war, with the trout swimming around me, head down, trying to nose into the bank to rub out the hook. After about ten minutes of this I lifted him out with my hand, having no net.

As I returned him, I can only guess at his weight but he was about 4½ or 5 pounds. A friend of mine, who hooked a 4½ pound brown trout one day on the Big Beaverkill below Roscoe said that it was in the net within a minute or two without ever knowing that anything was wrong until it was too late.

Of course, a big fish can be a different story in heavy water, such as the Pit or the Feather River in California, where I have frequently scrambled downriver in pursuit of a fleeing rainbow for a battle that left me nearly as exhausted as the fish. But in our more easy-flowing Catskill and New England streams, a trout of 1½ to 2 pounds seems to me the very best to catch. And I would greatly prefer a day in which the rewards were three or four medium-sized fish than one spent in pursuit of a single big one. The angler who has a passion for big fish only, at any cost, is missing a great deal of the charm of the sport by not simply taking things as they come. Fishing, to me, should be a relaxed pursuit, and the angler who hurls himself at his quarry, covering miles of water in a day or hotly stalking a single fish for an entire week end, will probably return to find me asleep on the bank after having watched his flying coat-tails disappear around the bend.

The Neversink taught me the true meaning of many things and I emerged from those experiences a more philosophical man. And both my wife and I learned much of angling from the many days spent on those clear waters under Mr. Hewitt's tutelage.

To Max, particularly, he imparted a practical knowledge of stream-craft, casting and fishing with a patience and interest equalled only by her appreciation. How much he had contributed toward making her an angler of prowess neither a big brown trout nor I realized until one day when I tried fruitlessly for an hour to deceive him. He looked over my fly a few times but each time turned it down with a nonchalance which was irritating to an already sorely tried angler.

When I finally decided to give up, Max, who had been waiting on the bank, waded out to try for him. Secure in the knowledge that if I could not get him after such long effort, she could not, I started off up the stream. I had gone but a few steps when I heard her reel screech and turned to see the fish slash madly across the pool. He had taken her second cast and thus two more males had underestimated the power of a woman.

CHAPTER XIX *My Favorite River*

THIS BOOK could hardly be complete for me without including something in its pages about the river which I love the best. For years my friends had fished it, had found good trout there and had extolled its virtues. My own introduction to this big, little river was not particularly favorable, except that I did readily recognize its possibilities. It took several trials before I began fully to appreciate its charm. It still remains to me, although I live near its banks and fish it nearly every day, the most difficult of rivers and yet the most rewarding in the things which count the most.

For a stream which appears placid enough, moving along its green valley in no particular hurry to join its parent river, the Hudson, it has a surprising weight of current and one learns to respect it accordingly. In early season it seems that I am usually in to the very tops of my waders; it calls for cautious footwork. The depth of water, surprising in a stream which appears rather small, makes possible many fine holding places for trout. And it contains the lovely long riffles which are such good insect producers.

A certain natural prejudice may be responsible for my belief that the trout of this river are gifted with a degree of caution rarely encountered in the breed, and it seems to me that no fish over which I have cast my flies offer more evidence of the cunning which makes trout such excellent game.

Along the upper river there is a great deal of water very nearly impossible to fish except from a boat or canoe, due to its depth and the heavily covered banks. This seldom-fished water acts as a reservoir of a sort—a source of stocking for the rest of the stream. Trout grow there nearly unmolested and move to new abodes when food becomes scarce or their numbers too great. At one or two places in this upper water it shallows so that it can be waded with caution. Frequently the angler must slide down a vertical bank the height of a man or more into water which is apt to be nearly up to the top of his waders. Then he must work his way along through a tangle of sunken logs, brush, deep pockets, mud bottom and such a host of other obstacles that, at least, he seldom meets anyone else doing the same thing. The trout are there and even on the warm summer days are apt to be rising. Casting to them offers real problems and in the clear water one can hardly make many mistakes.

One fairly long stretch permits decent wading. With the heavy cover on the banks and the arching trees overhead, it is like fishing in a green tunnel. The water is smooth and quiet, with only a spattering of sunlight finding its way through the leaves, and as you look up the stream you can see on the surface the little rings that the angler loves. Here the trout rise almost constantly every day. They are not large as a rule but occasionally you find a good one, and his length and bulk are all the greater by contrast.

The favorite flies here are the very smallest. We usually lengthen our leaders a bit by adding a few tippets of very fine gut and try not to make too many mistakes in our approach or presentation; it is embarrassing to see the wake of a good fish departing, due to some clumsiness. Here, too, the black flies and mosquitoes are apt to be abundant and hungry and this no doubt results in fewer anglers and better fishing.

A few years back, my fishing was cut off completely for a season because of a bad skiing accident and my only contact with the river was through the reports of my friends who kept me posted on what was happening there. The tales were both interesting and exasperating, as it was questionable fun to hear of the latest big one while lying in a body-cast, only a few hundred yards from the river. One day a pair of very excited anglers came to relate the latest exploit and it turned out to be something of no mean importance.

These friends of mine had located a large brown trout. Near the big deep pool where he lived was his feeding position, in about three feet of water, near a bank and under a fallen tree. Several tries for him at various times had failed to produce. They were curious to see whether he might be risen to a dry fly; they doubted it, but thought it worth a good trial. One day, one of them found the big trout out in his place near the bank and called his friend on the 'phone They both went down to try all their tricks in a determined effort to get him to rise; one would fish and the other watch from a prone position on the bank.

After considerable time spent in alternate trials and long rests, there was still no reaction; the big fellow was still there but appeared not to mind their attempts. Finally one put on a sort of hair mouse to see if the fish could be at all interested in a surface lure. Sure enough, he came up and looked it over, showing definite interest, but no take. That was encouraging, so they went back to their dry flies, and Walter Squiers, whose turn it was to make the next try, put on a big dun spider, or skater, very large and bushy.

On the second or third cast the big brown came up and took it solidly, as if he had planned the whole thing. For a moment neither angler could believe what had happened. However, both were soon very busy trying to get him out of the river, which was a problem as neither had a net. It was finally accomplished by a combination of kick, carry and run. When it was all over there was a grand fish on the bank. Just seven pounds, twenty-six and one-half inches of him; a handsome specimen. It hardly seems fair to give Walt the entire credit for that rather spectacular capture although he did hold the rod and hook the fish. It was Mead Schaeffer, my good friend and fishing companion, who gave himself a thorough soaking to get the trout ashore. Such teamwork certainly deserves commendation!

There is no minnow fishing allowed on our river in Vermont, which is perfectly agreeable to me, but last year I came very near breaking that law through no actual fault of my own. I had hooked a small trout of six or seven inches on a variant while fishing a good run, deep at the far bank where some bushes overhung the water. Bringing him in quickly so as to give him my blessing and let him go, I was about to reach out to pick him up when suddenly out of nowhere a great fish appeared and before I could realize what was happening, opened his long jaws and engulfed my trout in the wink of an eye. There was no hesitation or any other nonsense—he simply swallowed the little fish in one gulp. I very nearly sat down in the river, but when my line began to run out I felt I should at least have a try at hooking him.

The leader was 3x; I knew what might happen and sure enough, it did. At the first cautious tightening, the line fell slack and I reeled in a fly-less leader. Undoubtedly the teeth of the big fellow were responsible, for any fish of the size of that leviathan is apt to be supplied with dentition like a barracuda. Repeated attempts since then to bring my hefty friend up to a fly have been fruitless. I imagine he is still there unless dead of old age, for if a trout of that size were caught I am sure I would hear of it.

There are several of those "Aunt Sallies" in our river and they add a fillip to our fishing. Some have been risen a number of times, but rarely is one hooked. In almost every instance they break off or the little hook does not hold. Each season we approach their hides with a renewed curiosity as to whether they are still about. No doubt age accounts for some, but if the spot is a good one another large fish usually takes their place.

One such hideout was the object of continuous and applied effort on my wife's part. She had risen the fish several times without ever touching him, in each case to a big spider. The last day of the season we were on the spot and a parting try was being made before it was too late. I might add that my wife had definitely earmarked that trout for her own. She had located him, risen him and felt that he should be hers. I was careful to avoid anything that might resemble an encroachment on her property rights.

The hour before dark was spent in a variety of presentations but with no rise. I had taken down my rod and was standing on the bank as my wife turned and started for the shore with a sad and disappointed look.

"He must have moved his home," she said. "Better luck next year."

She had taken only a few steps when there was a tremendous splash across the pool under the bank and she turned to watch the rings widen over the dark water.

"He's still there, all right," she said, "but I wish he would have a little more respect for my feelings. At least he could have waited until I was out of sight!"

Downriver, over in New York State in a big flat where I have spent some interesting days, I once located three good fish, not really big, but respectable. This was in early season, and every day for a week or more we had enjoyed a hatch which brought the trout up well. The day I discovered these fish, two of them were risen and one hooked, but he came unstuck in a short time. The third fish wouldn't come to me at all, and I saw him rise only a few times to naturals. The next day I was back waiting for the hatch to come out. Sure enough, the little sailboats began to appear and shortly two of the fish began to show. I worked on one for a while, raising him once to a spider after he had refused a fairly good imitation of the hatch. I turned him over on the strike, so he went down for good. The other came to my fly so savagely that, as frequently happens, he did not rise again.

This sort of rise has had similar results many times in my experience, and I have often wondered exactly why it affects the fish so strongly. Possibly they frighten themselves with their very enthusiasm. At any rate, if one of these terrific smashes is missed, I have rarely been able to get the fish up again.

The third trout was fished for but didn't appear at all. Next day I was back again, and found all three rising sporadically. After a few casts to the most difficult one he finally rose, was hooked and eventually landed—a beautiful bright yellow trout, about seventeen inches long, with spots of vermilion. He took a fly of my own design which approximated the hatch reasonably well. The next fish was alternately cast to and rested for some time before he, too, came to the same fly, but the hook pulled out after a good run. By then the third fish had stopped rising and could not be moved.

The following day the hatch was not so heavy, but one trout was showing—the one lost the day before, I imagine—and I finally hooked and landed this fish after considerable effort. He was about the same size as Number One, and came to the same fly. The third and most obstinate fish of all, is, I hope, still there and I also hope to find him this season. The whole affair was a very interesting experience and I doubly appreciated the reasonable success after finding the fish so particularly difficult and choosy.

At another place downriver, this same hatch had caused several good trout to congregate in an eddy. They were able to feed with little effort as the flies came to them again and again in the current. The only places to cast from were the top and the base of a high, steep bank. If at the top, the trout saw me only too well, and if low, it made for difficult casting. Even from the low position, the trout could easily be seen as they came up to the fly. It was both fascinating and difficult to wait until they turned with the fly before striking. I missed a couple this way. The whole

business was somewhat humbling, as on one day I took only a single fish when at least a half dozen were rising. That day I not only tried several dry flies of proved efficacy but went to wets, nymphs, and all sorts of presentations. The next day resulted in taking six out of about a dozen in view, which was certainly better, but I never worked harder (nor ever had more fun, for that matter!). Since the eddy brought the naturals to the fish again and again, they could pick and choose the ones they liked. The eddy also caused a nasty drag on my leader and line. The spiders did not work well, either; it was one of the few days on which they were not taken by at least one or two trout.

I returned several days later and found that some of the trout had moved out of the eddy up into the current. I could reach them only by wading out well above, in the rather high water, and floating a fly down to them from upstream. The change seemed to agree with them that day, and I ended by taking all of three rising fish on a dry Quill Gordon. This left a better taste in my mouth, not from eating them, as they were all returned to the water, but from that infinitely more superior flavor of success.

We don't often find that birds are a handicap to our fishing, but one day in a long run which produced some excellent trout at times, I had an argument with a Cedar Waxwing that ended much in his favor. There are overhanging trees on the far side of this run and the deep water makes it difficult to get a fly over to where the fish lie. It frequently takes several attempts to put a fly in the right place, and when we bring off a good cast we are expectant of a reward. One day I was well out into the deep current, trying to place my fly across under the branches where the good ones lived. The fly was a large spider with nice stiff hackles, and I was confident that it would look good to a trout. There was a bird on a branch over the "hot spot," half hidden by the leaves, and I noticed that he became quite excited when my false casts approached the water nearby.

The first cast to the water was short of my objective, but fairly well over. The moment it touched, the bird—now I saw that it was a Cedar Waxwing—swooped down from his perch and picked it up. He flew up to the branch with it, held it a moment and then dropped it. I retrieved the line, made a couple of false casts with a somewhat startled comment, and shot it back again, this time right up near the bank where I wanted it. The blasted fowl was down on it in a second, picking it up again, this time dropping it before he regained his perch. The fly started to float and he picked it up again. By now I was wondering whether I hadn't better redesign my flies to be less alluring to birds and more to the fish, and said something to that effect in a loud voice. He sat there on his branch expectantly waiting for the next cast and when it came he picked it up again, and this time I'm sure, with a smirk on his face. I was convinced by now that no trout of any sense whatever would want that fly if he had to snatch it from the beak of a bird, so I reeled in and went away from there, reviling all birds in general and that one in particular. Thank heaven, that was the last I saw of him.

Not long ago I was exchanging some reminiscences with a good friend and angler, a medico of our town. He is a man of many experiences and has fished the river here when native trout, and large ones, were common. He told of how he had learned to fish the fly and of a man he fished with, an old-timer at the sport, who taught him the art and guided his ways on the stream.

One day when the two were out together, he had not been particularly successful while the old man had taken several fine fish. As they sat on the bank for a smoke and a bit of discussion, he asked his mentor what might be considered the most important things on which to concentrate his efforts, that he might eventually achieve such good results.

The old man cogitated for a spell, puffing on his briar. Finally he knocked it out on his heel and replied, "I believe we could boil it down to about three things which everyone can practice without wasting their time. And they ought to go about it like this: First, in casting, always choose a spot on the water and never use more line than is necessary to reach that spot. Second, always try to make each cast just a little better than the one before; and last, fish every riffle or pool as if it were the only one in the whole river."

The medico, I might add, has applied this teaching, and with good results. It seems to me that we could do worse than practice accordingly. There is a great deal in those suggestions, and if I were asked to name three better ones, I would certainly doubt my capacity to do so.

The objective of advice to anglers is twofold. If they profit by it, they catch more fish. If they learn from it that enjoyment of the sport for itself is just as important, they are tasting the full flavor of the angler's reward. The frustrations of inexperience can be discouraging, but the pleasure and gratification which go with intelligent practice will more than compensate. The value of experience is great, that of observation hardly less so, and the observing angler will go a long way toward reaching proficiency and the understanding of angling that gives to the sport its unique character.

No one angler will ever know all there is to know about fishing. It is one of the reasons why this sport is so universally popular. To the experimental and inquiring mind, casting a fly onto the stream is only part of a never-ending study of nature, the fish and his environment.

Legend for color plate **A**

DRY FLIES (Chapter IX)

NUMBERS 1 to 6 show the author's series of dry flies, standard tie
NUMBER 7   small dun or black variant
NUMBER 8   variant number 3 in text
NUMBER 9   spider number 2 in text

WET FLIES (Chapter X)

Showing numbers 1 to 5 in text

NYMPHS (Chapter XI)

NUMBERS 1, 2 and 3 show author's nymph patterns (three quarter top view)
NUMBER 4   Collins hard-bodied nymph number 1
NUMBER 5   Collins soft-bodied nymph number 2 (both shown three quarter top view)
All fly patterns are slightly larger than actual size

Legend for color plate **B**

SALMON WET FLIES (pages 174–177)

NUMBER 1	Silver Gray		NUMBER 6	Abe Munn "Upriver"
NUMBER 2	Blackville		NUMBER 7	Jock Scott
NUMBER 3	Cosseboom		NUMBER 8	Bastard Dose
NUMBER 4	Oriole		NUMBER 9	Squirrel Tail
NUMBER 5	Half-Stone		NUMBER 10	Mink Tail,
	(on low-water hook)			(on low-water hook)

SALMON DRY FLIES (pages 179–180)

NUMBER 1	White Wulff		NUMBER 4	Macintosh
NUMBER 2	Gray Wulff		NUMBER 5	Pink Lady Bivisible
NUMBER 3	Hunt's Teagle Bee		NUMBER 6	Stone Fly

STEELHEAD FLIES (wet) (pages 147–150)

NUMBER 1	Skykomish Sunrise		NUMBER 4	Queen Bess
NUMBER 2	Silver Ant		NUMBER 5	Harger's Orange
NUMBER 3	Thor			

(See text for classification of districts)